TIM BURT

The Author:

Helmut Merschmann is a freelance journalist who writes about subjects related to film and media in publications such as *epd Film, Berliner Zeitung* and *Frankfurter Rundschau*. He is multimedia author for the Berliner Filmmuseum on the Potsdamer Platz and wrote a PhD thesis on postmodernism in American mainstream cinema. His published essays include: 'Jules et Jim' (in a book on triangles in European avant-garde), 'Product placement' and 'History of film production'.

Dirk Schaefer lives in Berlin, where he writes and composes — mainly for films. In 1999 he was the first musician to receive the prize for experimental film at the European Media Art Festival in Osnabrück. His last work, the short film *Vacancy* (1999), in collaboration with Matthias Müller, was nominated for the European Film Prize.

Thanks:

I would like to thank my first readers, Carsten Fedderke, Unda Hörner and Orlando Busch, for their suggestions and advice, without which this book would have looked very different. Oliver Heisig of the *Videodrom* deserves many thanks for his experienced assistance, as does Constance Hanna for her support with the correspondence.

Helmut Merschmann

TIM BURTON

Helmut Merschmann

Translated by Michael Kane

TITAN BOOKS

TIM BURTON
ISBN 1 84023 208 0

Published by
Titan Books
a division of
Titan Publishing Group Ltd
144 Southwark Street
London SE1 0UP

First edition October 2000
10 9 8 7 6 5 4 3 2 1

Published by arrangement with Dieter Bertz Verlag.
Tim Burton © 2000 Dieter Bertz Verlag, Berlin.
English translation © 2000 Michael Kane.

Editorial team: Wiltrud Hembus, Maurice Lahde, Johannes Roschlau, Philipp Sperrle, Anja Wedell.
Photo sequences: Wiltrud Hembus, Dieter Bertz.
Layout: Katrin Fischer.
Special thanks for friendly help to Hans-Joachim Neumann and Sabine Rutkowski (*Zitty*), Robert Fischer and Herbert Klemens (Filmbild Fundus Robert Fischer), Peter Latta (Picture Archive of the Stiftung Deutsche Kine-mathek), Annette Stoffel (Constantin Film), Milan Pavlovic (*Steadycam*) and the Videodrom team — Bertz Verlag

Many thanks to Rory Mulholland and Niamh Warde for their advice in the initial stages of this, and to David Barraclough, Gillian Christie, Vanessa Coleman and Bob Kelly at Titan Books — Michael Kane

Did you enjoy this book? We love to hear from our readers. Please e-mail us with any comments at: readerfeedback@titanemail.com or write to us at the above address.

A CIP catalogue record for this title is available from the British Library.

Printed and bound in Great Britain by MPG Books Ltd, Victoria Square, Bodmin, Cornwall.

Contents

*Two clichés are ridiculous,
a hundred clichés are fascinating.*

Umberto Eco

The Draughtsman's Contract

An individual's handwriting is just as much a part of their identity as a fingerprint — handwriting is seen as a mirror of the soul. Graphologists claim to be able to draw conclusions about a person's character from their handwriting, and to interpret every squiggle as a facet of their personality. In law, an individual is seen to be represented by their signature. Handwriting reflects personality, and if we look back at old school books, we soon realise how much it changes over the course of time. Most of us consciously try to alter it at some point, and not just by practising signatures on rough paper. Such progress accompanies events in our lives — handwriting evolves as the character develops. How much more significant then is the 'handwriting' or the signature of an artist, the imprint of a film-maker with a unique view of the world and the opportunity to express himself. Tim Burton has always known how to unite aesthetics and autobiography, and to merge the development of his artistic expression with his *biographical project*, and to some extent reproduce the 'true' story of his life, and this distinguishes him from most Hollywood directors. Of course, caution is required towards the authorised biographies created in the dream factory. Only particular aspects of a life are revealed to the eyes of the public — only those which project the desired image and which help to increase the market value of the subject.

It is striking how single-mindedly Burton has taken elements of his life and his art and turned them into one cohesive myth, which actually seems to be

A striking resemblance: Tim Burton, during the shooting of *The Nightmare Before Christmas*, and Johnny Depp as Edward Scissorhands

less the result of Hollywood's notorious publicity machine than of his own self-styled *Wunderkind* persona. Burton manages to incorporate a certain reflexivity into his films which constantly refers back to his ongoing *biographical project* — some of his heroes are the spitting image of their creator, and many of the things that happen to them appear to be inspired by memories of his own childhood. The symbolism centres on the notion of the 'artist', an image which is in fact the product of these very leitmotifs.

Born 25 August, 1958, Tim Burton studied at the renowned California Institute of the Arts (Cal Arts), a hotbed of future talent for the visual arts in sunny Valencia, California. On the advice of a high-school teacher, the young student applied for a scholarship to the programme in animated film. Although he was just eighteen years of age, he showed considerable promise. Walt Disney was one of the founders of the school, where artistic ability was promoted, but at the same time it served to breed prospective employees of the Disney studio. Still rather unclear about his future career, Burton did know that it would have something to do with drawing.

Burton's early childhood had been relatively unspectacular — he grew up in 'Anywhere, USA', as he calls it, in Burbank, one of Los Angeles' many suburbs and home of the Warner, Columbia and Disney studios. He made afternoon trips to the cinema, watched B-movies on television and painted obsessively in his room. His lower-middle class parents had the windows facing the street bricked up, leaving only small slits to look through. According to legend, young Tim had to climb up onto his desk when he wanted to see out. Later he noticed parallels with Edgar Allan Poe's tales of people locked up in dungeons, or buried alive and facing death from thirst and asphyxiation.

While still quite young, Burton developed a penchant for horror and ghost stories, whose simple symbolism he found fascinating. It's not surprising then that the film versions of *Frankenstein*, *King Kong* and *Godzilla* were among his favourite works. Every American youth of his generation grew up with them. But *Scream, Blacula, Scream!* (1973, dir. Bob Kelljan), a blaxploitation film in the vampire milieu; *Dr. Jekyll and Sister Hyde* (1972, dir. Roy Ward Baker), a transvestite version of the legendary metamorphosis; and *The Brain that Wouldn't Die* (1963, dir. Joseph Green) — this was stronger stuff. The latter relates the story of a surgeon searching for a body onto which he might graft the head of his fiancée in order to save her life. The film evidently made a lasting impression on Tim Burton, and he referenced it as recently as *Mars Attacks!* in 1996, where the head of a female television reporter is sewn onto a dog's torso. Green's film, in which 'a guy's arm is torn off and he scrapes the bleeding stump along a wall before he dies, while a head on a tray laughs at him,' as Burton describes it in an interview, 'would no longer be shown on television today'.

Scream, Blacula, Scream!: Blaxploitation with Pam Grier, who later featured in *Mars Attacks!*

Heads that wouldn't die: Pierce Brosnan and Sarah Jessica Parker in *Mars Attacks!*

Burton's film career actually began when he was still at school, even if he never seriously thought about becoming a director. As a member of the American baby-boomer generation he grew up with television, and showed little interest in reading, not even comics. Burton submitted Super-8 films instead of written homework, and for a psychology course he produced an original clip (set to Alice Cooper's song 'Welcome to my Nightmare') in which he's attacked by a beanbag while sleeping. Due to the crude symbolism, every decent interpretation must fail, but he was still awarded a good grade for it. The amateur shorts he made later at Cal Arts were similar — in 1976 he shot a movie with a 'Mexican' monster and then a real Californian surfing film. You have to wonder what that looked like! Study at Cal Arts was strictly disciplined, almost like military service, but the students had every freedom in terms of subject, and could try out various techniques. As a fan of Ray Harryhausen and an admirer in particular of Harryhausen's animated sword battle scenes with miniature skeletons in *Jason and the Argonauts* (1963, dir. Don Chaffey), Burton naturally chose to try his hand at the classic stop-motion technique.

In 1979, Tim Burton was among those offered a permanent position with Disney. He was involved in drawing *The Fox and the Hound* (1981, dir. Art Stevens, Ted Berman and Richard Rich) but did not particularly enjoy the production line nature of the work. The chief animator, Glenn Kean, usually left him scenes with the cute little fox — with the result that Burton quickly developed an allergy to cute little foxes (the strange creatures which populate Burton's own films might help the reader understand the suffering it caused him). His first real challenge as a draughtsman and animator came with *The Black Cauldron* (1985, dir. Ted Berman and Richard Rich). As a conceptual artist, he enjoyed great freedom, and for an entire year he had nothing else to do but sit alone in an office and put everything in his head down on paper. He drew characters, series of movements, spaces and detailed sketches. On countless sheets of paper he produced work which would only benefit him in the long term — in the

Stop-motion tricks in *Jason and the Argonauts*

short term, the result was sobering. Not one of his designs was used in the final film. It was evident that Burton's approach was not in tune with the favoured style at Disney, and he described his situation there thus: 'I was very strange back then. I was always perceived as weird — I would sit in a closet a lot of the time and not come out, or I would sit up on top of my desk, or under my desk, and do weird things, like get my wisdom teeth out and bleed all over the hallways. I was kept at arms length, but at the same time they let me be. I guess I did enough work not to get fired. The company was in a kind of screwy stage at the time. They were making things like *Herbie Goes to Monte Carlo* (1976, dir. Vincent McEveety), and nobody knew what was going on there' (*Burton on Burton,* Mark Salisbury).

The great days of Disney as a family business were coming to an end. The structure of the company was out-dated, and it was unable to match the huge box office successes of the past. However, in 1984 Michael Eisner and Jeffrey Katzenberg brought a breath of fresh air to the kingdom. Eisner and Katzenberg were the men behind Touchstone Pictures, a successful subsidiary company which specialised in movies for the adult market. The overwhelming success of Disney's *Beauty and the Beast* (1991, dir. Kirk Wise, Gary Trousdale) under their management was the beginning of the Renaissance of the classic animated film. The two young moguls also initiated the further growth of the theme park empire into Tokyo and Paris, and brought about a flurry of expansion into a variety of activities in the video and television business, such as the founding of the Disney Channel, which, though initially a flop, became an enormous success. Traditionally concerned with creating totally unrealistic fictions, Disney has even been trying to merge illusion with reality. They have built an artificial model town, 'proper, clean and without social problems', near Orlando, Florida. 'Celebration', as the town is called, looks a bit like the setting of *The Truman Show* (1998, dir. Peter Weir) and, in the opinion of Michael Eisner, is a 'prototype for the coming millennium' (*Der Tagesspiegel*, 18/10/98).

Tim Burton arrived at Disney at a time when it was undergoing enormous change. The remains of the old glory days were still in evidence, and were part of the self-image of those employed there. They saw themselves as a community of artists, and it was not unusual for the company to employ people whose talents were promising, although not immediately useful. The young director was lucky — these days, the financial resources and creative pool of this world might not be so open to someone so off-the-wall as Burton, despite his obvious ability. At that time, it served him well. He found a niche for himself and his own particular bizarre imagination and, with the support and protection of the colleagues he befriended, such as Julie Hickson, director of the creative department there, he produced his first professional short film, *Vincent*, with a budget of just $60,000.

Vincent — A Spine-Chilling Homage

'**V**incent Malloy is seven years old, he's always polite and does what he's told, for a boy his age he's considerate and nice, but he wants to be just like Vincent Price.' So begins the voice-over at the start of this black and white film made in 1982. A combination of puppeteering and animation, it tells the story of a child who gets carried away by his imagination. The boy prefers to play with spiders and bats than with dogs and cats. Under his little feet the hall of the house is transformed into the tunnel of a ghost train. He wants to dunk his overweight aunt in a pot full of hot wax, and his dog Ebocrombi mutates into a monster during a scientific experiment with electrical energy. At night, the boy and his dog creep through the thick London fog, hunting for victims. Vincent avoids the light of day and prefers to stay in a darkened room, in spite of his worried mother's admonitions. He reads of Edgar Allan Poe's greatest fear — being buried alive — and he shudders. Left alone in the haunted house with the portrait of someone now deceased, Vincent has some sinister visions which, in the end, cause him to lose his senses. As he falls to the floor we hear a voice intoning a line from Poe's poem 'The Raven': 'And my soul from out that shadow that lies floating on the floor, shall be lifted NEVERMORE.'

This six minute-long hallucination is a fond evocation of the spirit of Edgar Allan Poe, but it's easy to see that it's also a respectful homage to Vincent Price. Burton peppered his first film with a range of quotations from B-movies in which Price played the principal role. Some of his motifs are derived from the

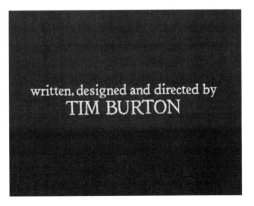

written, designed and directed by
TIM BURTON

Vincent's experiments with his dog, Ebocrombi

Roger Corman films *House of Usher* (1960), *Pit and the Pendulum* (1961), *The Raven* (1963) and *The Masque of the Red Death* (1964), all featuring Price. There are also references to other classic American horror films starring Vincent Price, which show Burton's enduring love of the genre, such as *House of Wax* (1953, dir. André de Toth) and *House on Haunted Hill* (1958, dir. William Castle). Burton has often expressed his admiration for this cult icon — the horror actor created his last screen character, an inventor and creator of life, in the Burton film *Edward Scissorhands*. Furthermore, drawing on his many meetings with Price, Tim Burton made a documentary film with the working title *Conversation with Vincent*, which remains unreleased. The parallels with *Ed Wood* — in line with Burton's biographical *raison d'être* — are evident. In *Ed Wood*, the 'worst director of all time' films the last touching scenes of a 16mm movie in which his hero, the heavily-accented Bela Lugosi, famous for immortalising the role of Dracula, breathes in the scent of a rose in front of his house.

Where does Burton's admiration for Vincent Price come from? It's probably to do with Price's acting style, with his gravity, seriousness and old-fashioned elegance in even the crudest scenarios. Vincent Price was inclined to grand gestures and liked to exaggerate his acting. He preferred to give too much of what was good than satisfy himself with less. This was utterly appropriate for the characters he portrayed; the refined aesthetes,

Dark visions: Vincent and the portrait

Vincent Price in *Pit and the Pendulum, House of Usher* and *The Raven*

withdrawn aristocrats or mysterious, possessed figures. His acting style, which veered towards the camp, became his trademark, a style which underscores the decadence of his characters and was, incidentally, something new to the classic horror film. A conspiratorial look about his eyes and the corners of his mouth betrayed an attitude never far from irony. His face was frequently hidden behind masks which his characters were constrained to wear after dreadful accidents or mutilations — in two of his most typical roles, Professor Henry Jarrod in *House of Wax* and Dr Phibes in *The Abominable Dr Phibes* (1971, dir. Robert Fuest), the characters even wore the face of Vincent Price as a mask hiding some hideous deformity. That particular device was camp through and through, and Tim Burton was one of its greatest admirers. Fascinated by the idea that only masks could reveal the true personality, Burton had stumbled upon an important theme for his later works: 'I discovered that when you put make-up on people, it actually makes them more free. They can hide behind a mask and show another side of themselves. Whether it be Johnny Depp in *Edward Scissorhands* or Jack Nicholson as the Joker — it's fascinating'(*Burton on Burton*, Mark Salisbury).

In *Vincent*, Burton gave us not only a first taste of the overloaded Baroque world of his imagination but also a glimpse of his own childhood, which he skilfully worked into the short narrative. Apart from the central motif of the murky depths hidden behind young Vincent's

neat and proper appearance, the story told off-cam-
era, a rhyming poem, is also influenced by the work of
Dr Seuss, a writer of children's books that Burton read
in his youth and much admired, and whose first pub-
lication *And to Think I Saw It on Mulberry Street* told
a very similar story back in 1938. It's about a boy who
keeps his thoughts hidden from his father in order to
avoid getting into trouble. The boy and his father
wander along Mulberry Street and perceive completely
different things from their different perspectives.
Unchecked by the reality principle of the adult, illogi-
cal, magical scenarios play out in the boy's mind. Tim
Burton has returned to this lack of inhibition and logic
in the childish imagination found in many of his films,
and this is very much a part of his biographical theme.
For two weeks *Vincent* was shown, not inappropri-
ately, as a supporting programme for Tim Hunter's

Tim Burton with Vincent Price during the
shooting of *Edward Scissorhands*

début film *Tex* (1982), a story about adolescence with Matt Dillon in the leading role. *Vincent* won prizes at film festivals in Chicago and Annecy in France, but the movie was soon forgotten, and it was only as supplementary material on the DVD/laserdisc version of *The Nightmare Before Christmas* that the short film made a reappearance.

With *Hansel and Gretel* in 1982, Burton made a variation of the Grimms' fairytale with an Asian cast for the newly founded Disney Channel. Like *Frankenweenie* in 1984, it was produced by Julie Hickson, but wasn't favourably received by either the high-ups at Disney or the critics, and was only broadcast once before being consigned to the archives. However, Burton's next television film, 1984's *Aladdin and His Wonderful Lamp*, received much greater recognition and was shown as part of Shelley Duvall's *Fairie Tale Theatre*, a series on the cable channel Showtime. This was Tim Burton's first opportunity to work with well-known actors — Leonard Nimoy (*Star Trek*'s Mr Spock) was the evil Moroccan magician and James Earl Jones played three roles, as the narrator and two ghosts. The design was seen as particularly impressive — in an underground cave, the props now familiar from the underworld of Burton's imagination make an early appearance: spiders, skeletons and other strange creatures, winding passages, distorted proportions — quite an Expressionist box of tricks.

Frankenweenie — The Monster in the Child

Frankenweenie, a black and white short film just under thirty minutes long, can be seen as Tim Burton's apprenticeship, though his mastery is already apparent. This movie was a *coup* for Burton and it was to lay the foundations of his reputation. He was just twenty-six years old, with a million dollars at his disposal. This adaptation of the Frankenstein myth, set in American suburbia, was planned as a supporting film for the re-release of *Pinocchio* (1940, dir. Ben Sharpsteen, Hamilton Luske). However, when *Frankenweenie* was finished, the *Motion Picture Association of America* (MPAA), the American board of film classification, gave it a PG rating, meaning that 'Accompaniment by adults is recommended; some scenes could be unsuitable for children.' This was extremely unusual for a Disney release and it effectively meant that the audience would be greatly limited. For this reason, *Frankenweenie* did not get a regular opening date. When Burton asked what was particularly objectionable about the movie, and what should be changed, he was told that the whole tone of the film was too sombre. It was only in 1992, after it had been praised at countless festivals, that the short work appeared on sell-through video and was shown on the Disney Channel.

Frankenweenie begins with a film within the film. Bursting with pride and enthusiasm, eight year-old Victor Frankenstein (Barret Oliver) shows his parents (Shelley Duvall and Daniel Stern) and a few friends a Super-8 film with the ominous title *Monsters from Long Ago*. The leading role in the short is played by the family dog, a bull terrier called Sparky. Both the dog's costume (he's dressed up to look like a primeval dragon-monster) and the partial anagram hidden in the title are allusions to Jack Arnold's *Creature from the Black Lagoon* (1954). The plot of Victor's short film is rather naïve — as smoke rises from an Indian tepee, a Tarzan doll sails across the screen on a bat attached to a fishing rod by nylon thread. The dog tries to snap at it and pulls the tent down. The End. Applause. Victor bows like a good boy. What happens next shatters the apparent harmony of the

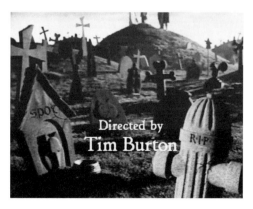

The film within the film: Sparky plays a monster

family idyll. During a ball game in the front garden, Sparky runs out on to the road and is knocked down by a car. He's laid to rest in the local pet cemetery. Victor is distraught, but has a brilliant idea when he sees how his physics teacher uses electric shocks to make the leg muscles of a frog contract. In bed at night, Victor devours that standard work *Electricity and the Creation of Life*, and the next day he secretly constructs a laboratory in the attic of his parents' house. After much waiting, a stormy night is forecast and Victor, or rather, Master Frankenstein, exhumes the dog and connects him to an apparatus consisting of lightning conductors, kites and hypnotic, spinning discs. The experiment is successful and Sparky is brought back to life. The dog is, however, somewhat the worse for wear — his body is covered with poorly-sewn seams which leak dramatically when he drinks. The poor creature must be kept hidden, but still the neighbours soon learn of the sinister occurrences in the Frankensteins' house.

A modern Prometheus

Frankenweenie is based on the novel *Frankenstein, or The Modern Prometheus*, which Mary Shelley wrote in 1818 at the age of eighteen. The progressive concerns of her novel, one of the high points of Romantic horror literature, distinguish it from the traditional gothic novel, which was entirely given over to the irrational and a macabre fascination with the uncanny. Shelley's approach is different — her monster is described sympathetically, not as something terrifying. The reader is not supposed to shudder in fear but rather to feel empathy, to identify. The monster is a lonely and misunderstood being. Rejected and despised by those around it on account of its outward appearance, it suffers unspeakably. The reader actually sees the creature as much less monstrous than its creator, Dr Frankenstein, and it is this sympathy with the persecuted creature which also characterises James Whale's two famous film versions of the story, *Frankenstein* (1931) and the sequel, *Bride of Frankenstein* (1935), which Tim Burton refers to in *Frankenweenie*.

'If you have a weak heart and cannot stand intense excitement or even shock, we are advising you not to see this production. If, on the other hand you like an unusual thrill, you will find it in *Frankenstein*,' advises the prologue of the first of Whale's films, thereby attempting to emphasise more than just the feeling of terror about to set in. Rather, the film concentrates on scientist Victor Frankenstein's internal conflict and on a negative utopia resulting from the consequences of the incipient processes of industrialisation and modernisation of society. Both the mad scientist and his creation, the test-tube creature put together out of parts of corpses, appear as necessary consequences of societal and technical development. They embody the unpleasant but inevitable side effects of the production of scientific knowledge, an amoral interference in the laws of

Creature from the Black Lagoon, *Frankenstein* (Boris Karloff) and *Bride of Frankenstein* (Elsa Lanchester, Karloff)

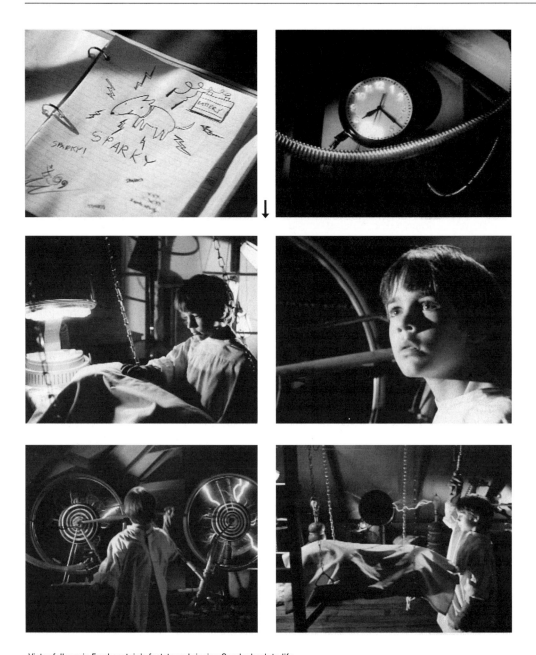

Victor follows in Frankenstein's footsteps: bringing Sparky back to life

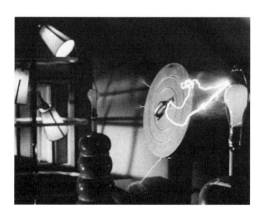

The mob takes up the chase

nature and of God. Added to that is the fact that Dr Frankenstein has committed two mortal sins, at least as the Romantics saw it: firstly, he has turned his back on society, and his chosen isolation naturally drives him to delirium; and secondly, he has abandoned his creation, the monster, and left it to fend for itself, denying it a father's guidance. That too must be avenged. James Whale uses a certain amount of poetic licence when he lends *Bride of Frankenstein* a gently ironic tone and shows the sensitive side of a monster who is only lacking the right kind of company — a woman.

In *Frankenweenie*, Tim Burton touched on another area of conflict described by the Romantics — the conflict between the individual and society. His film emphasises the reactions of the local people, the neighbours, to the artificial creature — hysterical reactions showing their lack of understanding for the alien and unfamiliar. These reactions are not without their funny side, though. There is an almost slapstick quality to the scene in which Victor, sensing some hostility in the air, wants to present the dog as a 'scientific miracle' on the advice of his father — a fight breaks out in the Frankensteins' living room, lamps fall to the ground, chairs are overturned, there is screaming and Sparky makes for the hills. The mob takes up the pursuit, which leads to a windmill on a crazy golf course where the dog has taken refuge — a clear reference to Whale's films. When the crowd sets the wooden structure alight with their torches and Victor tries to save the animal, tragedy occurs. Victor faints, and while Sparky manages to rescue the boy from the burning mill, he loses his own life (again) in the process. The mob then recognises the goodness in the monster, and he is brought back to life a second time with the aid of the concentrated power of several car batteries — 'Give 'em more juice', barks the fat neighbour (Roz Braverman) — and, like the monster in *Bride of Frankenstein*, Sparky finds his great love in the end, a lovely black poodle with a silver streak in her hair.

Just as James Whale produced a modern interpretation of Mary Shelley's novel, Tim Burton, for his part, was able to adapt James Whale's films anew and bring them up to date by combining two systems of symbols. Burton has stylistic recourse to the formal symbolism of the gothic novel, which he juxtaposes with the sober, functional world of American suburbia. The graphically attractive three dimensional appearance of the gravestones and crosses at the pet cemetery, the gently hilly scenery in front of the indirectly lit backdrop on the crazy golf course and the dark and stormy night of thunder and lightning accompanying the act of creation are all references to the classic motifs of fantasy films, deprived of their eeriness in Burton's movie. Horror is only present as a quotation and has therefore lost its effect; the dark scenery of the genre has acquired a Romantic cartoon appeal. This world of symbols encounters the equally familiar film set of a thoroughly planned and controlled suburbia, which makes young Victor feel he

A happy dog: the finale

is an outsider and needs to create for himself a companion, a friend — a monster.

Like all of Tim Burton's films, *Frankenweenie* is a homage to the cinema of terror and the sudden shock, to the aesthetics of the cheap thrill. With the aid of numerous stylistic references, like black and white photography, strongly contrasted lighting and games with shadows, as well as distorted perspective, he calls to mind both the disturbing Expressionism of German silent films and the classic Universal horror movies of the thirties and forties. Burton constantly harks back to this time, which was an almost mythical age of innocence in the cinema for him. People who pay no attention to his biographical odyssey, as discussed earlier, are often all too hastily inclined to explain his style as simply the result of an affinity for bad taste, for the trashier side of entertainment. Burton's perspective on past phases of popular culture, a perspective influenced by distance and irony, stems directly from something utterly personal. Who else could Victor be, if not Burton himself? Remembering the past and working it out — Tim Burton's reflections on the cinematic myths of his childhood and youth resemble the psychoanalysis of pop culture, therapy sessions too captivating to tear ourselves away from.

Creatures of the Day

All of Tim Burton's films feature one common theme, which may be described as an archetypal Romantic conflict — the confrontation between the inside and the outside, between the worlds of fantasy and reality. Burton's central characters create a world for themselves according to the design of their imagination, a world in which they live withdrawn lives. This artificial environment is the reflection of their inner selves, a real manifestation of the imaginary world of Burton's heroes. They are constantly trying to alter their surroundings aesthetically, to make them more beautiful and poetic, to assimilate them into their own imagination. Whether these changes are material or only notional, the outside world thus becomes a product of fantasy, a Romantic fiction... it becomes art.

Pee-wee Herman, for example, lives in a world of toys, a Legoland in which this boy growing out of his children's shoes can remain a child. He is sceptical of the outside world; he finds it threatening and uses sarcasm to deal with it. Or take Edward, with scissors for hands — he leaves his fairytale castle to go out among people, and proceeds to trim everything he finds there according to his own bizarre fancy — garden hedges, hairdos, ice sculptures and people are but clay in his hands, waiting to be transformed by his artistic creativity. Or Batman, the 'winged avenger' in his secret cave, constantly hatching out new plans to combat crime and avenge misdeeds. Batman's highly-tuned sensitivity to injustice is, fundamentally, aesthetically motivated. Taking the law into his own hands, his tidying-up operations aimed at crooks are intended to cleanse society, to

Aliens as artists: *Mars Attacks!*

liberate it from ugliness and upset. Another example is the cross-dresser, Ed Wood, driven to live out his secret vice — women's dresses and angora sweaters — to the great distress of those around him. His penchant for the peculiar is so pronounced that he even makes educational films about his predilection. In *Mars Attacks!*, extra-terrestrial beings, those creations of the human imagination, avenge themselves on their inventors — Martians attack humans. The aliens embody a fantasy which has left its former creators behind to lead an independent life of its own. One can find this particular allegory in every one of Tim Burton's films, and it's also a metaphor for art itself. For who, if not the artist, is being haunted by the spirits he has conjured up?

In constant conflict with the outside world, Burton's heroes are virtually possessed by their own imagination, as if it were an alien force. They are fanatically obsessed with realising their vision and come to grief in a world which can only look at them with incomprehension. Then these characters either withdraw and turn their backs on the world or are driven out and find a home in their original paradise. Burton's protagonists are outsiders who take pleasure in their non-conformist roles. 'I'm a loner, a rebel,' Pee-wee Herman says conspiratorially to a girl whose affection he wishes to deflect. 'There are things about me you wouldn't understand. Things you couldn't understand. Things you *shouldn't* understand.'

Even outwardly, Burton's characters don't quite conform, and they are beyond the scope of their surroundings in both

Outsiders and eccentrics: Burton's heroes in (left) *Pee-wee's Big Adventure, Beetlejuice, Batman*, and (right) *Edward Scissorhands, Ed Wood* and *Mars Attacks!*

Suburbia in *Frankenweenie...*

appearance and behaviour. Either they carry some kind of stigma that renders them monstrous, like Edward Scissorhands, or they deliberately dress conspicuously and extravagantly, like transvestite Ed Wood. These eccentrics and odd characters transgress the norms and ideals of society and test the tolerance of their surroundings. A young post-punk with scissors and knives instead of hands? A grown man who dresses up as a bat and wears a rubber cape? A director who steals his girlfriend's angora sweaters because this is the only way he has of feeling close to her? A deceased couple who haunt their own house, scaring off the living? This is a truly bizarre tribe.

On closer examination, one realises that the lower-middle class idyll Burton's characters enter looking for contact and attempting to reconcile themselves with 'the world' is no less strange than they are themselves. It's only those for whom this is normality who don't notice how bizarre it actually is. However, for the outsider, from whose perspective we are shown the world, 'normality' looks quite different. For example, through Edward Scissorhands' view of suburbia we see a monotonous street meandering through an estate where the houses are as similar to each other as one egg to another, their different pastel shades feebly trying to create an impression of individuality. People's lives are restricted to their carefully tended front gardens and polite contact with the neighbours. In the morning, as if in response to a secret command, the husbands set off in their cars and proceed out of the estate in a convoy to pursue a tedious, pen-pusher's career somewhere. Their wives all wear the same clothes and hair-styles, perform the everyday household chores and stock up on rumours. They all seem to be imprisoned in the same dreary routine which cries out for something to break its eerie monotony.

Tim Burton requires only a few takes to sketch out a grotesque version of the American ideal of equality and community. He only needs to exaggerate a little to make the familiar seem strange to us. And thus we see the picture of a treacherous idyll, threatening to implode at any moment — the latent terror slumbering in this place is just waiting to show its face. Betrayal and intrigue, evil machinations and secret vice, hot desire and ice-cold calculation hide behind the prettified façades and surfaces of normality.

Of course, Burton is not suggesting any real social criticism here — his films are far too unconcerned with reality for that. Their refuge is fantasy, defined by the conventions of cinema and popular fiction, like the strict delineation and opposition of good and evil, beautiful and ugly, as well as genre and narrative conventions such as the happy ending. Burton plays such clichés and rhetorical devices against each other, or more precisely, he misuses and undermines them. He wants to draw attention to what Baudelaire called the 'blank refusal' of reality, a reality which represents a constant offence to the imagination and which can only be reconciled in fiction and in the cinema. This act of will requires an individual and unique act of imagination, the invention of a totally new world.

...and *Edward Scissorhands*

Pee-wee's Big Adventure — A Trip into the Ego

If *Frankenweenie* signalled the start of Tim Burton's career, the commission to direct *Pee-wee's Big Adventure* was a well-timed follow-up project. Paul Reubens, a successful television star in his time, came to see *Frankenweenie* through an agent who was friendly with Burton, and he looked on the young director as a congenial comrade-in-arms. The affinity between the two is evident in a common theme in Burton's short films — the discrepancy between self-perception and outward appearance — which is also the central theme of *Pee-wee's Big Adventure*.

In the early eighties, Reubens had his own television series on the American broadcasting network CBS, *The Pee-wee Herman Show*. It was later transformed into *Pee-wee's Playhouse*, a regular programme for children which ran from 1986-91. The original series was aimed at older children and young adults, and quickly acquired quite a cult following, with its weekly afternoon offering of colourful craziness. Pee-wee Herman, the character created by Reubens, is a pubescent teenager ready for any kind of fun and with a fondness for breaking the rules of taste and behaviour. He wears little mirrors on the tips of his shoes in order to be able to get a glimpse under girls' skirts, for example, and is full of suggestive remarks ('I said ear, not rear!'). Guests on the show were willing victims for smutty jokes of all kinds as Pee-wee Herman sublimated his awakening sexuality into childish talk and games.

Paul Reubens as Pee-wee Herman in
Pee-wee's Big Adventure

The subsequent variation, *Pee-wee's Playhouse,* was milder in tone, if no less anarchic. The props included a talking window and an armchair that could hit out wildly; all the participants and spectators had to shout out at the top of their voices at the mention of an agreed

Over the top: *Pee-wee's Playhouse*

word, which was changed constantly — hysteria and exuberance were the order of the day. The autonomous life of objects became the trademark of the show, which included short film sequences, stop-motion clips and puppets as well as the comedy sketches.

Pee-wee Herman himself was the main attraction, however. With his tightly-cut light grey suit, white shoes, red bow tie and rouged cheeks, Reubens gave his character a hint of androgyny (and also referred back to Harry Langdon, a famous comic actor from the twenties). As an adult playing a child's role without sexual connotations, it left many questions open — questions which are of no importance in *Pee-wee's Big Adventure* and are ignored by all the other characters. While his androgynous appearance was in line with a trend of the time, androgyny was then only accepted in pop stars, and it certainly wasn't common on children's television. It was ironic that the peculiar sexuality which had been bracketed off in the *Playhouse* broke out beyond the programme and brought about a sudden end to Paul Reubens' career when, in 1991, he was denounced for indecent exposure in a porn cinema and the press jumped on the story, haunting him. After that, he disappeared from the screen for a while, but continued to do voice-overs for various animated film characters, including Lock in *The Nightmare Before Christmas*, and he made a guest appearance, hidden behind a moustache, as the Penguin's father in *Batman Returns*. Reubens was also present at the MTV Awards in 1992, but his own television career seemed to be at an end. There was an uninspired sequel to *Pee-wee's Big Adventure* called *Big Top Pee-wee* (1988, dir. Randal Kleiser), which was significantly less impressive than the first film in terms of grotesque ideas, and was also much less successful.

Pee-wee's Big Adventure deals with the obsessions of a boy whose beloved bicycle is stolen and who embarks on a long odyssey to recover it. There are suggestions of parallels to Vittorio de Sica's classic film

Ladri di Biciclette (1948, aka *Bicycle Thieves*), even if there is little of his neo-realist approach to be seen, since the *cinema povera* has long made way for a cinema of affluence with huge budgets at its disposal. While Burton may have little to do with any kind of social realism, he has been impressed by one renegade of neo-realism, Federico Fellini: 'I think I always liked Fellini movies because he seemed to capture the spirit and the magic of making a movie... He created images that even if you didn't know what they meant literally, you *felt* something' (*Burton on Burton*, Mark Salisbury). It is perhaps only in Fellini's later works, like *Ginger e Fred* (1986) and *Intervista* (1987), that an obvious connection can be traced, but one can assume that his earlier works must have had an influence on Tim Burton too. One thing they have in common is an affinity for the fantas-

Pee-wee and his deluxe bicycle

Pee-wee's marvellous kitchen appliances

tic; for creating a wondrous, imaginary world which promises all the freedoms of the imagination. While Fellini revered vaudeville, the world of jugglers, magicians and small-time artists, Burton shows similar respect for his horror icons and Romantic characters. Both directors have used their work to deal with the conditions of making a film and with the notion of creativity as a motivation for (artistic) existence, and both have employed the film-within-a-film technique. Furthermore, their work is full of autobiographical traces, clearly referring to their individual artistic and social backgrounds (which, incidentally, could hardly have been more different).

Fellini, however, presented his protagonists at a stage of personal failure, a typical theme of modernity which he associates with the collapse of traditional models of masculinity: 'That which has been achieved is never comparable with that which has been wished for, longed for, desired. Far away hills remain far away' (*filmdienst*, 24/1993). Whereas for Fellini the constant feature of subjectivity is always recognisable in the real world, Burton dispenses with this social grounding. He is also interested in failure, but as a deliberately constructed conflict, a Romantic gesture revealing the irreconcilability of the individual and the world. Nevertheless, Burton's characters are artistic creations through and through, products of the imagination whose environment is merely a backdrop. Over the course of his career, Fellini withdrew more and more from the daylight of the street into the dark world of the studio, but the artificiality of that set-up didn't affect his humanist concerns at all. One could say the same of Tim Burton's career — *Pee-wee's Big Adventure* features the most location scenes of any of his films, and Pee-wee Herman's ontological condition in the real world seems unexplained in many ways. Just as Fellini maintained the world within the studio, Burton sustains the degree of artificiality and symbolism of this particular odyssey.

An odyssey against all odds

Pee-wee Herman's home is a pop-art wonderland, a colourful villa indiscriminately stuffed with toys and all kinds of useless gadgets and gizmos. In the morning, the breakfast apparatus gets under way — while Pee-wee is washing himself in the bathroom, the automatic fried egg machine starts to clatter in the kitchen, oranges press themselves and a plastic archaeopteryx swoops down to drop two slices of bread into the toaster. At breakfast, Pee-wee has a brief chat with the two fried eggs and rasher of bacon — which look like eyes and a mouth — on his plate before he gobbles them up and flies out of the door. Bursting with anticipation, he keys a secret code into the electronic door opener of his garage and then we finally behold his pride and joy, a revamped red and white child's bicycle, a Schwinn, the Harley Davidson of push-bikes. He polishes the chrome surfaces proudly until he can see his face gleaming in them, and then sets off for the city to buy a few things. It's in the city that he loses his bicycle when he leaves it attached to a suspicious-looking toy clown with a steel chain of almost infinite length.

This disaster leads to a search tying together several loosely connected episodes. First, Pee-wee rounds up his friends, neighbours and acquaintances and makes a long and tiring speech reconstructing the probable course of events in minute detail. He seeks advice from Madam Ruby (Erica Yohn), a fortune teller, and is told to go to the Alamo in Texas — named after the fateful location of a particularly bloody episode during the conflict between Texas and Mexico — because his bicycle is supposedly hidden in the cellar. Pee-wee sets out on his long journey, hitch-hiking. On the way, he meets Mickey (Judd Omen), an escaped prisoner whom he helps out of a scrape while dressed in women's clothes. Later on, he is picked up by Large Marge (Alice Nunn), the long-distance truck driver and terror of the highways, who takes him some of the way. Pee-wee subsequently learns that she actually died in a fatal accident ten years earlier, and that he must have been dealing with her ghost. Shortly after, while in Palm Springs, he meets Francophile waitress Simone (Diane Salinger), with whom he spends a night in intense conversation which strengthens her resolve to go to Paris and angers her pot-bellied boyfriend Andy (Jon Harris). When Andy threatens him with a dinosaur bone, Pee-wee jumps on a moving train and ends up singing eerily beautiful folk song duets with

Pee-wee on the road

a tramp. Having finally arrived in the Alamo, the cradle of Texas, he learns that the building doesn't even have a cellar. Announcing his business in the middle of a guided tour, Pee-wee is greeted with roars of laughter. Deeply saddened, he decides to head for home, defeated. Later, he barely manages to escape being beaten up by a pack of Hell's Angels calling themselves 'Satan's Helpers' by dancing a two-step in platform shoes on the bar counter for them, melting the hearts of the rowdy Texans with this charming interlude. When the group cheerfully acknowledge him as one of their own and present him with a motorbike for the rest of his journey, Pee-wee promptly causes an accident and is escorted to hospital.

Purely by chance, he spots his missing bicycle on television — it's now the property of a blasé young boy

The chase through the film studios

in a television series. Pee-wee immediately breaks off his stay in hospital and sets off for Hollywood, repeating his odyssey in reverse. This time, it's Pee-wee himself that's the object of the search when he manages to steal his own bicycle back from a soundstage in the Warner Brothers studio, the security people are called in and a chaotic chase across several movie sets ensues. In full flight, Pee-wee sets some animals free from a burning zoo film shoot. In the meantime, the real bicycle thief has been caught and Pee-wee's great adventure is to be used as material for a movie (the film-within-a-film device again). However, Pee-wee doesn't play the lead in this action-adventure based on the James Bond model, only the small part of a hotel worker. Our hero finally gets his well-earned fifteen minutes of fame at the première, held in a drive-in cinema. In the final scene we see him — or rather, his shadow projected on the screen — riding away on his bicycle.

Has Pee-wee, the eccentric youth, thus become a mature, recognised member of society? The story is based around the tradition of initiation — the arduous path through adolescence and the final entry into the world of adults. Ritual tasks have to be accomplished, along with tests of endurance which demand staying power and intelligence. Everything revolves around sexuality — the beloved bicycle, the object of Pee-wee's obsession, represents a desired person, but at whom could Pee-wee's desire possibly be directed? He makes peace with his friend Dottie (Elizabeth Daily), who mothers him, but they don't marry and she doesn't become his partner. Was the long trip across America perhaps in the end a symbolic journey to the self, Pee-wee's gay coming out? Only by means of camouflage has he managed to win through against bikers and bandits, spiteful local boys and ugly rituals, and thereby achieved at least temporary social acceptance. The film appears to conclude with the suggestion that the conflict between the individual and society may only be resolved by means of affirmation — through outward

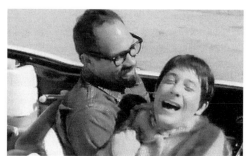

Camouflage: Pee-wee fools the police

conformity at the expense of inner integrity. Just as Pee-wee's experiences on his journey are smoothed over and falsified when they are filmed for Hollywood, so can he only achieve social acceptance through a kind of play-acting, a masquerade of masculinity.

Pee-wee has to play the strong man and prove himself via activities seen to be manly, but he utterly subverts the process and does it in a thoroughly un-masculine fashion. Thus, he dances to avoid being beaten;

wears women's clothes to help the escaped prisoner pass a police checkpoint and would much rather flirt with him than with any girl; and has a satisfying conversation with Simone, the Francophile, instead of seducing her. Withdrawal into the world of his own imagination remains the only escape from a reality he has found to be corrupt and wrong-headed.

Stylish stubbornness

It was thanks to a happy coincidence that Tim Burton came to direct *Pee-wee's Big Adventure*. Paul Reubens had seen *Frankenweenie* at a film festival and was enthusiastic, sensing that he had a great deal in common with the young director. Without hesitation, he suggested the hitherto unknown novice as his preferred candidate to direct the Pee-wee movie. According to Burton, although he was not involved in drafting the script of *Pee-wee's Big Adventure*, his own immediate affinity with Pee-wee Herman, the outsider, meant a lot to him. Burton was particularly fascinated by Pee-wee's obsessive love for an ordinary object — the stolen bicycle — which meant absolutely nothing to anyone else (similar protagonists populate Burton's later films, of course). Of crucial importance to Burton was the freedom he was given regarding the design of particular scenes, and he was able to use this freedom to create extravagant, over-the-top scenarios. The scene in which Large Marge, the trucker, briefly transforms herself into a terrifying ghoul with bulging eyes and a

Large Marge's scary metamorphosis

horrible grimace in front of Pee-wee's eyes illustrates Burton's fondness for stop-motion animation. Likewise, the pursuit through the Warner Brothers studios clearly carries Tim Burton's signature, as he slipped in a few elements of his own fledgling career; the Japanese director filming the battle between Godzilla and Ghidrah is reminiscent of the film at the beginning of *Frankenweenie*, for instance. There are also other allusions to Burton's early beginnings as a film-maker, like the surfing film and the music video for a heavy metal band.

In spite of the commercial success of *Pee-wee's Big Adventure*, largely the result of Paul Reubens' popularity at the time, Burton got bad reviews. The film appeared on some top ten lists of the worst films of the year. As Burton later recalled, one critic even remarked: 'Everything is wonderful, the costume design is brilliant, the photography is faultless, the script is fantastic, the actors are all good. But the direction is dreadful.' Tim Burton had to listen to this criticism repeatedly, especially as his subsequent films were also not without their weaknesses. For him, the devil is not in the details but in their sum — in the problem of chronological order and logic. Burton is fascinated by details, and his movies are packed with imagination, but they do tend to be somewhat episodic.

In *Pee-wee's Big Adventure* the structure, basically a succession of sketches, could be explained away as the influence of the stand-up comedian, Paul Reubens, but this same structure is used in all of Burton's later films too. Critics have repeatedly pointed out that Burton frequently sacrifices the story for the sake of the visuals, and that he sets too much store by impressive production design and costumes at the expense of coherence and psychological depth. But what is the attraction of Burton's films, if not precisely this atmosphere of live-action cartoon? *Pee-wee's Big Adventure* is early proof of Burton's stylistic confidence and stubbornness.

Edward Scissorhands — A Romantic Fairytale

Over the course of his career, Tim Burton had to pay dearly for his vision; up to this point, his films had been commissioned productions — as was *Batman*, the film which made him respectable, and, in particular, *bankable*. The enormous financial success of this huge blockbuster gave him a free hand in his subsequent projects. While all his films show the typical Burton touch, as patented by *Beetlejuice*, to some extent, Burton really unleashed his imagination for the first time when he made the pop fairytale *Edward Scissorhands* in 1990. Just as Burton's success is associated with *Batman*, his aesthetic reputation is inextricably linked to *Edward Scissorhands,* the film in which the artistic signature of the director is most clearly evident. *Edward Scissorhands* also counts as one of Burton's 'personal' films, personal in the sense that here he returns to his main theme, the fundamental Romantic conflict mentioned earlier, and once again brings in elements of his personal development.

Edward Scissorhands can be read as a dark, romantic fable for adults, another take on the disparity between the individual and society, on the unique nature of one single character and the horror of conformity. The Frankenstein story provides the model here, as it did for *Frankenweenie*, which could be described as a shorter version of *Edward Scissorhands*. 'I always loved monsters and monster films. I was never scared, I simply loved them, for as long as I can remember. My parents say I watched everything, and these things are still part of me. *King Kong, Frankenstein, Godzilla, Creature from the Black Lagoon* — they're all quite similar, and only really differ in terms of

costume design and make-up. There is something special about this identification — every child reacts to particular pictures, particular images from fairytales, and I found that most monsters were completely misunderstood. They usually had more sensitive souls than the human characters around them,' Burton explained (*filmdienst*, 24/1993).

'A monster with a heart' was one of the central themes of Mary Shelley's *Frankenstein*, with an emphasis on sympathy, and intellectual and emotional identification particularly characteristic of English Romanticism. In Shelley's work, the strange creature shows his sensitive side when he encounters people who are well disposed towards him; when he secretly observes the family who later teach him to speak, and to read and to write, for example. The fear of others, of society, and its rejection of him is the catalyst that causes the creature to turn on it, becoming the projection of the hatred directed against him — and thus a monster. *Edward Scissorhands* takes up this tradition in so far as the creature becomes an object of sympathy and makes the world around him appear monstrous in comparison with his own innate goodness. In Shelley's story, the ingenious father of the monster, Victor Frankenstein, is also drawn into conflict — because he has artificially brought about the miracle of life, he stands opposed to a society whose rules he doesn't recognise, and thus himself becomes an outsider.

Burton sets his story in a contemporary American suburb. The film opens on a winter evening with a classic fairytale framing device. Asked by her granddaughter where snow really comes from, a grey-haired grandmother replies that it's a long story, and proceeds to go way back to begin at the beginning. She recalls the unusual and fateful love of her youth, somehow connected to the castle which can just be seen through the window, far away on a mountain. The old lady's story must have taken place at a specific

Beauty and the Beast: Edward (Johnny Depp) and Kim (Winona Ryder)

time, when she was a young girl, but the aesthetic of the film is somehow timeless. Burton mixes classic design elements from the past, present and future; nineteenth century science is juxtaposed with colourful sixties decor, and the gothic meets the suburban.

It's clear who is really doing the remembering in *Edward Scissorhands*. In a photograph taken on the set, Tim Burton stands in front of Edward Scissorhands, giving directions to actor Johnny Depp. The resemblance between director and character is suddenly strikingly clear — even their hair is the same. But the autobiographical subtext of *Edward Scissorhands* refers less to Burton's own youth than to the fictions which influenced him; the stories, films and television programmes — aesthetic systems Tim Burton grew up with and was clearly fascinated by. Naturally, Burton has modified the imagery he absorbed — he describes this process as 'filtering through remembrance' — creating a world viewed through the mirror of personal recollection, in which objects acquire a distorted and often grotesquely magnified significance.

Childhood and youth are generally seen as the 'formative years' of our lives. Consequently, Burton has given each generation represented in *Edward Scissorhands* its own system of symbolic shorthand representing the different eras they grew up in, different times associated with different tastes, each expressing a particular aesthetic. The parents' generation is characterised by familiar fifties and sixties icons; the conformist, consumer-led boom of those years represented by lava lamps, functional interiors and social rituals like the barbecue. The younger generation wears the insignia of the eighties: jeans, T-shirts and the dream of fast money symbolised by a Landrover decorated with flames, all very reminiscent of the familiar aesthetics of Slacker films. Ultimately, Edward represents two apparently disparate cultures. His clothes — a tight black leather suit with metal accessories — look like the rebellious uniform of punk, whose 'no future' attitude and rejection of bourgeois society were actually directly descended from the self-isolation and self-obsession of the Rom-antics as embodied in our lonely, misunderstood hero.

Avon calling

An Avon rep by the name of Peg Boggs (Dianne Wiest) trawls for customers in the quiet suburb where she lives with her family. Peg isn't exactly flushed with success, and she is sitting, somewhat discouraged, in her car when she spies the old castle high up above the suburb in her rear view mirror and decides to try her luck there. The grounds turn out to be in surprisingly good condition, and the garden is full of shrubs carefully trimmed into strange shapes, including an enormous open hand. Peg enters the castle and climbs the stairs around the old walls. In the attic, she finds a timid creature with knives and scissors instead of hands, and he immediately inspires the sympathy of this undaunted woman with her mission to bring Avon to everyone. Using her cosmetics, she gives the boy's wounds some makeshift first aid and takes him home with her in the car. The news travels through the community like wildfire as the women gossip about the new arrival on the telephone.

Edward becomes *the* topic of conversation, and he makes himself useful around the neighbourhood. His skills at cutting and chopping make preparing

Peg Boggs (Dianne Wiest) on the way to the castle

Daring creations: Edward makes himself useful

salads for a barbecue a breeze, and his scissors are ideal kebab skewers. The next day he gives lap-dogs for miles around exotic new haircuts, and then moves on to their owners — the women adore their daring, asymmetrical New Wave creations. Edward gives Mr Boggs (Alan Arkin) a hand cutting the hedges and, working at lightning speed, creates giant sculptures of Godzilla, a portrait of the Boggs family and a dancing, joyful girl.

Edward starts when someone opens a tin with an electric opener during the preparations for the barbecue, and he becomes pensive. A flashback follows, explaining Edward's peculiar past. He remembers the hour of his birth, when his father, an inventor (Vincent Price), gave life to him. The creation scene takes place in a workshop in the cellar of the castle. A steam-driven machine hisses and clanks away, stamping out Christmas biscuits on a conveyor belt. The inventor holds a heart-shaped biscuit against a metal doll, and Edward's symbolic birth takes its course. The conveyor belt is a nod to *Modern Times* (1936), Chaplin's critical comedy about progress and the fundamentally problematic relationship between man and machine, and it also reminds us of the laboratory of Dr Frankenstein, where an experimental synthesis of man and dead material is produced which is ultimately bound to fail. Burton provides several flashbacks throughout the film, illustrating, for example, how the inventor tries to teach his creation social etiquette from an old-fashioned manual: 'Etiquette protects us from embarrassment and shame.'

Edward also receives instruction from Mr Boggs, who endeavours to show him how to conform to the rules of modern society and how to tell the difference between right and wrong, which Edward finds quite difficult. In response to the hypothetical question of what one should do upon finding someone's wallet, Edward suggests giving the money to friends. Later on, Edward is caught by the police taking part in a break-in, during which his skill and naïveté is exploited by people who want to use him and lead him into trouble. It is his lack of a conventional consciousness of injustice which leads to his being marginalised — access to society is denied to anyone who cannot distinguish between the rule of law and anarchy. This indicates a moral lacuna — the mechanisms of social control have not yet been laid down in the monster, and he has no identity as long as he has not been broken in. A raised index finger of warning is the traditional gesture Edward's strict teachers fall back on.

Talking about hands — hands are significant symbols throughout the film. When Peg Boggs comes across a prospective Avon customer, she makes conspicuously artificial hand movements suggesting the process of applying make-up but also resembling the elaborate gestures of an air hostess demonstrating a safety routine. Boris Karloff's timeless interpretation of

the monster also features peculiarly expressive hands, thrusting out from jacket sleeves which are much too short. In the second of James Whale's Frankenstein films, *Bride of Frankenstein*, the first image we see after the framing narrative is a pair of hands appearing behind a fissure in a rock as long, white fingers hesitantly feel their way along the cold stone. Hands symbolise the act of creation; they can form beauty, transform nature into art. But they can also destroy.

The last flashback in *Edward Scissorhands* shows Edward receiving a pair of human hands from his father as a Christmas present. These hands are the finishing touch to the inventor's creation, and his creature will be complete at last, ready to go out into the world. Edward is thrilled and tenderly runs the blades of his scissors along the artificial fingers. Suddenly, a look of pain and

Edward's creator (Vincent Price) in his laboratory

An unbridgeable distance: Edward and his father

fear crosses his father's face, as if he has seen his own death. Edward's clumsy scissors pierce the delicate hands as he panics, and they fall on the floor. When his father also sinks to the ground, it isn't immediately clear whether Edward has in fact killed him, and it begins to look as if Edward must destroy everything and everyone he loves. Frightened, he reaches out to stroke the cheek of the dead man — and his sharp blade cuts deeply into his father's face, drawing blood.

When Edward is looking for some form of closeness, the distance that separates him from other people remains unbridgeable, in direct proportion to the length of his scissors. The scissors can create astonishingly beautiful works of art, but they are also a hazard to human beings. This opposition of closeness and distance, affection and rejection, creation and destruction, was Tim Burton's starting point: 'The idea came from a drawing I did a long time ago, a picture I liked. It came

The artist and his model

to me unconsciously and had to do with a character who wants to touch, but can't, who is both creative and destructive... It came from the feeling that your image and the way you are perceived by other people are often completely at odds with what you actually feel inside' (*filmdienst*, 24/1993). The director expresses this discrepancy between appearance and reality in a scene in which Edward is presented as a curiosity on a television talk-show, struggling to answer questions from a prying

studio audience. When asked about his love-life, he becomes visibly upset and tongue-tied, staring into the camera without saying a word. Kim (Winona Ryder), the Boggs' pretty, blonde daughter, is sitting at home in front of the television. Edward has fallen in love with her, but has not yet been able to touch her heart. As he stares unremittingly into the camera, however, the object of his devotion gets the message.

In the lead-up to the budding romance with Kim we

57

are shown how Joyce (Kathy Bates), the neighbour, is bewitched by Edward's 'ambrosia salad' and provocative clothes. Her desire is inspired by the fact that he is different, and by his unique hands. 'Do you imagine those hands are hot or cold?' she asks a friend at the barbecue, 'and just think about what a single snip could do...' To which her friend replies: 'Or *undo*.' For Joyce, Edward's metal handicap promises a new kind of experience and perverse pleasure. She seizes the initiative in the back room of a hairdresser's salon, and when Edward flees, the tide has already begun to turn against him. Up to this point, the narrative has followed roughly along the lines of *Beauty and the Beast*, revelling in charming, kitsch set pieces, like the scene in which Edward uses Kim as a model for an ice sculpture. His angel revolves to the music of a glockenspiel, while flakes of ice and snow whirl around them. The artist and his model — a union as inappropriate and inevitable as Cathy and Heathcliff in William Wyler's classic 1939 film version of Emily Brontë's novel *Wuthering Heights*. This is the first and last time Edward manages to overcome the distance between himself and another human being and give a form to his affection — through his art. The fairytale atmosphere surrounding them doesn't last for long, however. The angry mob is already approaching to drive the monster back to the castle and separate the doomed lovers forever.

The framing fairytale closes with Kim, now grown old, telling her granddaughter that Edward is still in the castle, making ice sculptures as a sign of his love, and that the snow falling to earth is created by his work. With this symbolic act, Edward turns around the story of his own birth and transforms himself from a creation into a creator, thus acquiring one of the most important human gifts — the ability to express himself and exercise power over the production of meaning. It's true that he has to pay the high price of isolation, but this is the price every artist has to pay — at least according to Tim Burton's vision.

Batman Returns — The Mask Behind the Face

In 1991, after some initial reluctance, Tim Burton decided to take on the direction of *Batman Returns,* the sequel to his enormously successful *Batman.* However, he only agreed to do the film after modifications were made to the characters which he hoped would allow him a greater degree of control over the material. Burton had some bad experiences on the first *Batman* film in 1989 as a result of the pressure for success, not least because of the huge advertising campaign, which forced him into making compromises. With *Batman Returns,* he wanted to make amends for some of the previous movie's shortcomings. The template for the sequel had already been fixed by Warner Brothers, and the *Batman* sets were still stored in London's Pinewood Studios, but Burton didn't want to film there again, as too many bad memories were associated with the place. Sometimes, one needs a second run at things in order to get them absolutely right, and Tim Burton's ambitions had not quite been fulfilled by his

work on the first *Batman* project. Above all, he was dissatisfied with the way that the ambivalence of the characters, which caused them to switch constantly between good and evil, had been left underdeveloped: 'The psychological profile of many characters — the Joker, Catwoman, Harvey Dent — is easy to identify. But characters such as the Penguin and the Riddler are more complex. One wonders, "Who are these people?" And it's this notion of not knowing who we are which is the attraction of the *Batman* material for me' (*filmdienst,* 24/1993).

So, with the aid of scriptwriter Daniel Waters, Burton concentrated on providing *Batman Returns'* characters with a suitably schizophrenic duality. The sets teem with monsters and masked figures — the souls of the former are jet black, concealed beneath an everyday disguise, while the latter conversely put on the mask of a monster to prevent their souls from being damaged by the world. They are, however, all outsiders, even if they live in the midst of society and take their place within it. Their masquerade, a leitmotif of the *Batman* films, is the result of some personal tragedy which has made the characters what they are — personalities literally split right down the middle. The second *Batman* film deals explicitly with a monstrous world in which the ego and the id go their separate ways.

One of these evil yet tragic figures is the Penguin (Danny DeVito), who came into the world as the deformed child of rich parents, with fins instead of hands. (Just like Edward Scissorhands, his handicap is the source of the distance between him and the rest of the world.) The very first scene shows his painful birth; at night his horrified parents secretly throw the newborn baby into a river which flows into the drains of Gotham City. Penguins fish him out and raise him until, at the age of thirty-three, he feels the need to return to the surface. Full of hatred for the middle-class world which rejected him on account of his abnormality, he resolves to get his revenge by making them subject to his will. The Penguin makes his move while the city's politicians and industrialists are gathered on the Plaza for the celebrations to mark the lighting of the Christmas tree. He abducts the man who effectively rules the city, businessman Max Shreck (Christopher Walken), and in return for his release, Shreck has to introduce him into the upper echelons of Gotham society from which, despite his birthright, he has always been excluded.

While the Penguin was corrupted by his bad experiences, Max Shreck is one of the 'real' villains. A capitalist who knows all the tricks, he uses clever camou-

The Penguin's election campaign
(Danny DeVito)

flage to hide his treacherous intentions behind a mask of bourgeois respectability; he has no desire to provoke the public against him and the face he presents to the world is that of the successful entrepreneur and patron. He pretends to be interested in the well-being of the city while secretly hatching his own plans, aided and abetted by the politicians he has long had in his pocket. Schreck truly earns his name, borrowed from the actor who plays Dracula in Murnau's *Nosferatu — Eine Symphonie des Grauens* (1922), and which also means fright or terror in German. He plans to construct a new kind of power station which will suck in and absorb energy instead of producing it — a stroke of genius, particularly since his own company is one of the main suppliers of power to the city. The Penguin seems like an answer to his prayers, and Shreck artfully feigns an interest in his new acquaintance's ambitions for the office of mayor. In truth, the wretched Penguin is only a pawn in a much bigger game, being used as a decoy to distract the public from what is really going on.

Shreck's personal assistant, Selina Kyle (Michelle Pfeiffer), is another of the outlaws. Her sudden transformation into the leather-clad Catwoman is astonishing, since she is first seen as an inconspicuous character. The colourless secretary is unhappy with her career. Selina feels she is destined for higher things, but has to accept temporary defeat when she confronts her boss and informs him that she has seen through his scheme, after which Shreck throws her out of the window. A preposterous, comical metamorphosis, typical of Tim Burton, takes place, in which she is transformed into a cat with eight lives left. Along with Batman himself (Michael Keaton), the Catwoman is actually one of the good characters quite evidently wearing a mask to adopt a second identity, just as an actor slips into another role. They are thus able to explore the dark sides of their souls, the mirror image of the bright, public front, where all inhibitions are relaxed. As a representative of the 'weaker sex', Selina Kyle metamorphoses into a

The birth of the Catwoman: Selina Kyle (Michelle Pfeiffer) and Max Shreck (Christopher Walken)

Illusion: Christmas in Gotham City

strong, sexy woman wielding a whip. Her transformation is symbolised in a scene in which she has a fit of temper, damaging the pink neon sign in her living room in the process so it no longer displays the friendly message 'Hello there', but the more ominous 'Hell here'.

This shift of meaning and emphasis, represented by damage to the physical surroundings, is perhaps characteristic of the entire film, which repeatedly conjures up a particular atmosphere only to destroy it.

The events take place at Christmas, the festival of love and reconciliation celebrated even in Gotham City. But all the prescribed harmony is soon revealed to be a delusion, a deception which collapses in on itself. Lies and deceit lurk everywhere behind the façades, and nobody knows what anybody else is up to and who is in league with whom. Only one thing is certain: all signs have been uncoupled from their previous meanings and are only there to lead one astray. What is apparently a Christmas present becomes a hazard to the public when masked men ride out of it on motorbikes and fire into the crowd with automatic machine pistols. With perfidious pleasure, all the children's toys are blown into the air, and when a young blonde woman dressed as a festive bunny girl is about to switch on the Christmas tree lights, thousands of startled bats fill the sky. The Penguin then seeks the sympathy of the population by announcing publicly that he forgives them, declaring, 'It's human nature to fear the unusual,' but we can be sure that he isn't being totally sincere. It seems rather more likely that what the 'unusual' Penguin has in mind is a few lessons in real fear.

The only moment of truth takes place, ironically, at a masked ball to which all of Gotham City's important people have been invited. Among the guests are Bruce Wayne and Selina Kyle, the only two who are not wearing masks. They got to know one another, and were attracted to one another, while disguised as Batman and Catwoman. As they dance, their cover slips:

Wayne: 'I'm sorry about yesterday, but I had a pretty big deal going through — fall through, actually.'
Kyle: 'It's okay, I had to go home and feed my cat.'
Wayne: 'So, no hurt feelings?'
Kyle: 'Actually, semi-hurt, I'd say — There's a big comfy California King over in... What do you say?'
Wayne: 'Are we gonna take off our costumes?'
Kyle: 'I guess I'm tired of wearing masks.'
Wayne: 'Me too.'

The mask as a second skin: Catwoman, alias Selina Kyle (Michelle Pfeiffer), and Batman, alias Bruce Wayne (Michael Keaton)

Kyle: 'Does this mean we have to start fighting?'

Only now does the fight really begin for the couple, and it doesn't lead to a happy ending. They have been taken over by their alter egos for too long and can't now leave behind the freedom they have grown used to. For Selina particularly, the Catwoman disguise is more than a second skin, and the mask has become her true face.

Batman Returns deals with the conflict between centre and periphery, between the ordinary world of the

average citizen and the underworld of the outsider. But Tim Burton no longer strictly delineates the two, as in *Pee-wee's Big Adventure* and *Edward Scissorhands*, but rather shows them meeting, or colliding. In so doing, he reveals the time and the effort involved in attempting to rediscover the lost innocence of a society within its media images and representations, only to find the shattered pieces of a world once imagined as whole. Tim Burton is clearly fascinated by these fragments and

The architectural visions of Le Corbusier and Harvey Wiley Corbett...

reflections. His pop culture doesn't attempt to clear all the contradictions of society out of the way. On the contrary — in *Batman Returns*, these conflicts take shape and are, to a certain extent, personified. The film clearly distances itself from the narrative cinema of Hollywood and its 'realistic heroes', whose task it is to persevere through disharmonies or indeed to dissolve them. Here, the contradictions are shifted to the different facets of the characters' personalities and become alter egos instead.

The world as a theme park

The wintry *mise-en-scène* in *Batman Returns* is like the inside of a giant snowstorm, a fairy tale landscape where it's snowing softly. As in the first film, the cityscape is based on Manhattan, which has come to be seen as the archetypal modern city of the twentieth century. Manhattan has constantly been an inspiration to the imagination of countless architects who have lent this metropolis its monumental vertical form, reaching for the skies — a symbol of progress run rampant. Ever since the division of the city streets into blocks and the creation of the Manhattan Grid in 1811, this place has represented *the* great project of modernity: the perfect exclusion of chance, chaos and nature. Manhattan was to be a city without a shadow, an urban fiction tending towards science fiction. They had to build upwards because of the restricted space, and a dense forest of skyscrapers of a hundred storeys and more quickly grew. It was only the invention of the elevator which permitted this conquest of vertical space — in fact, the two 'fathers' of the skyscraper, Hugh Ferris and Harvey Wiley Corbett, imagined there would be bridges and arcades connecting the buildings at altitudes of hundreds of feet. Ultimately, that wasn't necessary, of course, as each individual sky-scraper constituted a complete block, a city within the city. The fascination exerted on film-makers by this metropolitan phantas-magoria is evident, from Fritz Lang's *Metropolis* (1926) to Syd Mead's immensely influential urban design for *Blade Runner* (1982, dir. Ridley Scott).

The Dutch architect Rem Koolhaas claimed that every calculation is the result of a secret desire, and that even the greatest rational effort is the expression of the col-lective subconscious. In his book *Delirious New York* he reads the city as a landscape of desire, an expression of imagination which exercises a 'constant conspiracy against the realities of the outside world'. Strangely enough, the architecture of Manhattan began with the amusement parks of Coney Island. The nature reserves originally intended for the recreation of stressed city dwellers soon became a miniature Man-hattan, which began to have an influence on its actual model. Three of the most famous parks — Steeplechase, Luna Park and Dreamland — were perfect experimental models for town planners such as Frederic Thompson and William H. Reynolds, who pur-sued their obsessive ideals there. Illusory places came alive with thousands of towers and minarets, illuminat-ed by millions of lights, 'functionless, apart from over-whelming the imagination and keeping any kind of recognisable, earthly reality at a distance' (*Delirious New York*, Rem Koolhaas).

In Dreamland, the amusement park 'for all classes' built by Reynolds at the beginning of the twentieth cen-tury, catastrophes such as earthquakes and train crash-es were simulated, and there was a miniature version of the Swiss Alps as well as a Lilliputian town called Midget City, not dissimilar to the underworld of the

...and Moses King (c.1900)

Coney Island

Penguin, in which it was possible to experiment with moral conventions — promiscuity and nymphomania were the order of the day and eighty per cent of the population was born outside of marriage. The dwarves even had aristocratic titles in order to heighten the affront to the Victorian visitors who observed the freaks in horror. In the Incubator Building there was an 'Institute for Child Breeding' (already seen at the World Exhibition in Berlin in 1896), where abandoned children were raised by the state, another parallel to the Penguin's upbringing.

In these spectacular amusement parks, grotesquely distorted illusions were declared reality. It is not surprising that Koolhaas is able to demonstrate that these parks influenced the architecture of Manhattan, the city which, despite its strict geometry, is also concrete evidence of the desires and hallucinations of its builders. Le Corbusier's 'obsessive' rational dreams devised a place which would exclude all reality, a master plan made real, in which the hubris of his pretensions is as obvious as the contradictions which were to blossom in Manhattan. It is, however, clear today that the atmosphere of this city is determined much less by rigorous modernity than by the many excrescences which no plan can provide for, and which render every calculation unreliable.

Luna Park

Midget City

The urban design of Gotham City closely resembles such a dream (or nightmare) landscape. The cityscape of *Batman Returns* can be read as a reflection of the schizophrenia of the characters within it. Bo Welch, *Batman Returns'* production designer, was able to borrow from a great variety of architectural styles, from Expressionism and Cubism to Fascist Modernity. Fragments of these styles, reflecting in their very variety the characters themselves, are to be encountered everywhere. 'What they built for the first movie was formal and serious,' Welch explained. 'This set is a little more American — it has a lot more wit and irony. The look of the city is influenced by sort of Fascist World's Fair architecture

Max Shreck's headquarters

mixed with generic American urban decay and a sprin-
kling of our more contemporary, profane mixed zoning'
(*Cinefex*, 8/1992). While the powerful, like Max Shreck,
are seen in impressive surroundings — monumental
buildings with ornaments in front of them reminiscent
of Nazi sculpture — the ordinary people, represented
by Selina Kyle, live in an untidy environment, overloaded with scenery. Evidently, the naïve pop design is
a reflection of the manipulated soul of the people. The
crowd scenes, such as the gatherings on the Plaza, are
accordingly provided with all the kitsch décor of
Christmas. The Penguin's home, on the other hand, in
a cathedral-like cave under a deserted park called
Arctic World, is furnished with elegantly curved Gothic
arches and dark vaults. However, Bo Welch was sure to

The Penguin's caves

avoid the one dimensional equation of style with identity, and paid some attention to breaking with each characters' trademark design elements. Thus, there is a touch of pure Art Deco in Max Shreck's head office, some hi-tech design in Selina Kyle's pink room, and the Penguin floats around his cave in a giant rubber duck.

Although Welch built a model of Gotham City which required Warner's largest soundstage and was even more monumental than the model city constructed by Anton Furst for the first film, the metropolis in *Batman Returns* appears less cold and brutal; it can even look almost homely. That's because no scenes are played in harsh daylight, and only rarely is a big, panoramic view of the whole city shown. The events largely take place in enclosed spaces, and even the Plaza feels as if it's

Selina Kyle's room

Gotham City Plaza

contained or surrounded by a glass dome. When the exterior becomes the interior, the world is turned inside out, as it were, and there is no difference between the surface and what lies behind — the strangest things occur in a place without boundaries. The physiognomy of the city mirrors the dubious features of its inhabitants, whose deepest secrets are similarly trying to get out. The giant Moloch, which changed its name several times over the course of the *Batman* saga (in the original Bob Kane comics, it was called Manhattan first, then Metropolis and finally Gotham City), is an upside down reflection of the shattered, kaleidoscopic spiritual landscapes of its citizens.

Sleepy Hollow – Heads Will Roll

Chop! The air screams as a sword cuts through it. A head falls to the ground, the eyes wide in panic. The now headless body belongs to a coachman driving a carriage along a dark forest road in full flight from a sinister figure, all in black, on a huge black horse — the Headless Horseman. The hunt covers virtually impassable terrain through the dark undergrowth. Barely a ray of light from the overcast sky penetrates to the ground, swathed in a wispy layer of mist. The leafless trees, branches whipping the face of the coachman, have something ominous about them. Anyone familiar with Tim Burton's movies will notice similarities to the dense wood in *The Nightmare Before Christmas*, just like the scarecrow standing at the side of the road with a Halloween pumpkin grinning maliciously on its shoulders is another of Tim Burton's horror trademarks stamped on *Sleepy Hollow*.

The year is 1799. For weeks, the quiet nest of Sleepy Hollow has been plagued by a mounted demon, and the police department of New York is very concerned. They have no way of explaining the horrific murders taking place north of the Hudson river, which have so far claimed four lives. Or, more precisely, five, if one includes the unborn child of a beheaded woman — as Constable Ichabod Crane (Johnny Depp), sent out into the province to investigate, soon discovers.

Crane's approach to the unexplained occurrences is strictly scientific — there must be a *reason* for the strange events amenable to the laws of logic and deduction.

We hear the 'chop!' several more times during the film, and see the heads severed at a stroke fall to the ground with an audible plop. It's hard to determine the body count exactly. In any case, the number of deaths is quite high for a Tim Burton film, and everyone in Sleepy Hollow is beginning to worry. Fear has taken hold of the little place where the houses cling to each other for protection and the family trees intertwine with each other... who will be the next victim of this sinister executioner? Of course, not everybody is a target for the horseman, as we later discover.

Ichabod Crane tries to keep a cool head during his investigations, even if he becomes queasy at the sight of the dead bodies. The handsome officer forces himself to be rational and refuses to believe in any of the ghost stories he hears in Mayor Baltus Van Tassel's house, where the town's most repected figures have gathered. He hears the legend of the Headless Horseman, a mercenary from Hesse sent by German princes to fight on the British side against the Americans in the War of Independence. Deriving great pleasure from carnage of any kind, the mercenary was delighted to set out for battle mounted on a black stallion, with his cape billowing behind him and his teeth sharpened to fangs. 'It made the blood freeze in your veins just to look at him,' explains Van Tassel (Michael Gambon). It wasn't until the winter of 1779 that the revolutionaries were able to put an end to his savagery, cutting off his head with his own sword. However, for some time now, according to the village elders, the monster has been at his evil work again, risen out of hell to look for a suitable head for his headless shoulders. Ichabod Crane will have nothing to do with this hocus pocus — he asks the gathering whether anyone has ever actually seen the horseman in person, but no one answers. Crane can no longer have complete trust in the credo 'seeing is believing'.

Crane's scientific approach is regarded with contempt by the villagers, who prefer to believe in ghost stories, and when he has the corpses exhumed to perform autopsies with his own home-made instruments

Enter reason: Ichabod Crane (Johnny Depp) arrives in Sleepy Hollow

The Headless Horseman...

the townspeople are scandalised. During his examinations, Crane wears a special pair of glasses with a built-in magnifying glass and telescope. He works skilfully with an awkward knife and uses chemical powders which leave a lot of smoke behind. It is clear from Ichabod Crane's excited activity that science has only recently been emancipated from metaphysics. He gets a great fright while out walking when he meets the black rider with a Jack-o'-lantern stuck on his sword. On this occasion the rider is actually only Brom Van Brunt (Casper Van Dien), out to scare the stranger who's been making eyes at his girlfriend. A little while later, however, Ichabod encounters the real rider in the forest, and witnesses a real beheading. He has to spend the following few days in bed, trembling like a leaf and stammering to himself, 'It *was* a headless horseman, I saw him.' Lesson one: seeing *is* believing.

When Crane first arrived in Sleepy Hollow, he walked into a party in Van Tassel's house, where they were playing a game. Wearing a blindfold, the daughter, Katrina (Christina Ricci), touches the stranger and, to the great annoyance of her boyfriend, Brom, seems to be very keen on him. A few scenes later, Ichabod shows her an optical illusion — a cardboard disc pulled taut between two threads, with a red bird on one side and a cage on the other — explaining to her that 'truth is not always appearance', and a typical Burton romance begins. If the cardboard novelty spins fast enough, the bird appears trapped in the cage. Whether this symbolises the mystery of love or Crane's profession is not clear — in any case, and this is lesson two, appearances are not always to be trusted. The scene is introduced by a colourful dream sequence in which a woman (Lisa Marie) twirls amid a flurry of cherry blossom in an elaborate landscaped garden. The parallels to the scene in *Edward Scissorhands*, where the beautiful Kim dances in the swirling snow, are underlined by the blonde wigs

Christina Ricci and Lisa Marie wear in *Sleepy Hollow*, as well as the stigmata on Ichabod's hands. As we later learn, the woman in the dream sequence is Crane's mother, who was tortured to death by her jealous husband in an Iron Maiden — in order to save her soul, according to the hypocritical morality of the time. This also explains Crane's call to science, to 'reason and truth': 'I was seven when I lost my faith.'

The pastel-coloured garden scenes stand out conspicuously from the otherwise pale spectrum of colours in the film, with acid green predominating. One American critic felt that Rick Heinrichs' production design left him with an impression of being 'washed-out and diseased' (*San Francisco Chronicle*, 19/11/99). In fact, the whole film hangs between the quotation marks of the Gothic horror aesthetic, which Burton pays homage to with great attention to detail in *Sleepy Hollow*. Unlike the tongue-in-cheek deconstruction of genre in some of his early works, in *Sleepy Hollow* he deals in earnest with the horror film — Christopher Lee's appearance is a clear signal that this is indeed the distinctive Gothic horror of Roger Corman and Hammer Studios. Like Corman's adaptations of Edgar Allan Poe's work, *Sleepy Hollow* is concerned with an internal horror, a horrific vision born of the naïve imagination and the pre-scientific awareness of the unsophisticated village dwellers. While the film does contain some pretty bloody images, the emphasis is not really on these murderous scenes but rather on a progressive attempt to show the historical conflict between Enlightenment and Romanticism.

...at work

Trick or treat

The film's plot is based on a literary model, 'The Legend of Sleepy Hollow', by Washington Irving, 'found among the papers of the late Diedrich Knickerbocker' (Irving's pseudonym), as the subtitle of the narrative informs us. Along with 'Rip Van

Blind man's buff: Johnny Depp, Christina Ricci

Winkle', it's considered to be one of the first classic American short stories. Irving was a lawyer, born in New York in 1783, who had devoted himself to literature with a passion. He travelled to Europe a few times, and spent a period in Germany, where he came across the old folktales which inspired many of his stories. For 'Rip Van Winkle' in 1820, he drew on the folk legend 'Peter Klaus' from Otmar's *Volks-Sagen*, occasionally without any alteration at all, but it has to be said that he still created his own mini-masterpiece. It's not surprising that Tim Burton was interested in the influential horror story about the supernatural horseman, especially as the American Halloween tradition is based on it, and Burton had used the iconography of Halloween quite recently in *The Nightmare Before Christmas*. Burton's approach to the conflict between Enlightenment and Romanticism, between a rational, scientific approach and the world of the uncanny and fantastic, is somewhat different from Irving's. For Irving, the romance between the poor teacher Ichabod Crane and the rich landowner's daughter Katrina Van Tassel was central, and also materially motivated. Burton is at best peripherally interested in Christina Ricci's character, whom he shows to be both an angel and a vamp.

This epochal conflict is crystallised in the character of Ichabod Crane, the intrepid policeman whose mind may not always obey the rules of reason, but who nevertheless strives to put his rational theory of deduction into practice in criminal investigation. From A follows B — at heart, Crane is an early detective, a worthy precursor of Sherlock Holmes and Auguste Dupin. It's largely due to Johnny Depp that the film manages to maintain a humorous edge without becoming just another silly black comedy. As he did in *Ed Wood*, Depp is able to show the complexity of a man pulled in different directions by his emotions and ambitions — an egocentric character from whose imagination the whole story might have sprung. The character calls to mind, as Depp jokingly suggested during an interview, a 'fragile young girl,' a combination of Angela Lansbury's Miss Marple in *The Mirror Crack'd* (1980, dir. Guy Hamilton) and the 'ethereal quality' of Roddy McDowall (*Salon* 18/11/99). Certainly, Tom Stoppard's (*Shakespeare in Love* [1998, dir. John Madden]) uncredited rewrite has given a touch of humour to Andrew Kevin Walker's (*Se7en* [1995, dir. David Fincher]) script, which, in accordance with the genre, had been written as a detective film but was not yet quite Burton-like. It's difficult to deny that *Sleepy Hollow* is, simply in terms of narrative, the most coherent film so far from a director with a reputation for paying little heed to narrative.

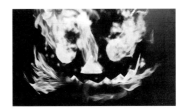

Birth of a myth: a mysterious rider with a Halloween pumpkin

The visual style is also convincing, and Tim Burton shows himself to be in full control of his artistic, creative power. If there's one film that looks almost as if it has been painted on a canvas, that film is *Sleepy*

Hollow. With the certainty of someone walking in his sleep, Burton employs the appropriate cinematic resources and rises to a new level of mastery in the set design. Influenced by the Hudson River school, a suggestive dream landscape unfolds in front of our eyes, animated by a sublime, convincing naturalness; by trickling streams, flame-yellow suns suddenly appearing between thick banks of cloud, endless fields and dark, dark woods. The landscape breathes melancholy and radiates indolence and energy in equal proportions. The set design evokes an intense, intoxicated power of observation, as if every possible sensation had to be included in each frame. Carried by the elegiac melody of Danny Elfman's score, the film luxuriates in the transport of its own opulence. It is Burton's best work so far, and one could hardly imagine a more suitable director for this material.

In *Sleepy Hollow*, Tim Burton has, of course, once again woven in a dense web of references to his other films and his *biographical project*. No one would be surprised by the fact that the main protagonist, Ichabod Crane, is another outsider in a closed, sometimes hostile, community. What is a little surprising, however, is that he wins his princess fairly effortlessly. In spite of this happy ending, Burton has remained faithful to his principles — to tell a sinister tale for adults, and not to shy away from violating cinematic conventions where necessary. Even small children aren't safe. When the murderous horseman hunts down a family in a farmer's cottage, a small, red-haired boy, whom we had previously seen playing with a magic lantern, projecting shadows of pumpkins and bats on the wall, hides in the cellar. Light penetrates the gaps in the floorboards so that the boy is able to pinpoint the position of the horseman above him. We are almost sure that the boy is going to survive, when the monster bursts through the floorboards with an axe and we hear the familiar 'chop'... just one example of how Burton throws convention overboard.

Nature with a soul (Johnny Depp, Christina Ricci, Marc Pickering)

When Ichabod Crane has recovered from the shock of his encounter with the beast, played by a convincingly possessed and raging Christopher Walken, of whom *Time* magazine wrote that he could frighten little children 'just by singing "I'm a little teapot"' (*Time*, 22/11/99), Crane decides to get to the bottom of the matter. He heads off into the forest, following the trail of the horseman, and his path leads him to a cave where a witch prepares a drink from the blood of a freshly-killed bat. As she sips it, the old woman undergoes the same kind of dramatic transformation we saw in the eyes of Large Marge in *Pee-wee's Big Adventure*. Finally, Crane arrives at the grave of the horseman, the enormous, twisted 'Tree of the Dead'. Blood is still dripping from a fresh wound in a root. On his way there he is joined by Katrina Van Tassel, and the couple watch the sinister horseman ride right out of the tree, the 'gateway between two worlds', on his way to satisfy his bloodlust.

Crane uses his powers of deduction and eventually puts two and two together, writing the words 'secret', 'conspiracy' and 'points to' in his notebook. It gradually becomes clear to him that the horseman himself is being controlled by a greater power. A murder plot is uncovered, and revealed to be the work of Van Tassel's wife (Miranda Richardson), who wants to get her hands on her husband's sizeable inheritance. She has long since changed his last will and testament in her favour, as we saw in the opening scene of the film, when hot sealing wax was dripped carefully onto a folded legal document and stamped. This stylish gesture, the distinctive stamp, shows the signature of Tim Burton the artist, and we, the audience, are the ultimate recipients of his beautiful and chilling dispatch.

B-Movies in the Mainstream

'**B**' is for basic, bread and butter or bottom of the bill, but it isn't normally associated with contemporary, mainstream films. B-movies were most frequently found in the American cinema of the thirties and forties, when they competed for the second slot in popular double features. During this period, one had the expensively produced A-film with opulent sets and famous stars, supported by the low-budget B-film without any big names. The major studios all maintained such production-line departments, but B-movies were more typically produced by small, independent studios which didn't have their own screening outlets, like Monogram or Republic, specialising in cheap product and launching one film after another into the market in rapid succession. Bought in by established Hollywood studios as gap-fillers and gingerly (if at all) picked up by the critics, B-movies never enjoyed much of a reputation. They dealt with genre material of all kinds and were always made according to the same simple formulae. Their aesthetic quality (or lack of) was determined by practical considerations — tight deadlines and small budgets influenced the final picture more than anything else — usually characterised by basic storylines and sets, low-tech lighting and often wooden acting.

Nevertheless, the ranks of the B-movie sometimes turned up the odd gem. In the horror genre, for example, Austrian exile Edgar G. Ulmer made the classic *The Black Cat* (1934), with Bela Lugosi and Boris Karloff, for Universal before he had to take his place on poverty row; RKO producer Val Lewton, of Hungarian origin, made masterpieces of subtle terror such as *Cat People*

Bela Lugosi and Boris Karloff in *The Black Cat*

(1942) or *I Walked With a Zombie* (1943) with director Jacques Tourneur; and one-eyed director André de Toth made *House of Wax* (1953), an early 3D film. In the fifties, as the hey-day of the supporting feature began to decline, Roger Corman was much talked about as one of the most financially successful makers of B-movies. His later colour, widescreen Edgar Allan Poe adaptations, starring Vincent Price, are legendary, and he had an equally impressive knack for spotting young talent like Francis Ford Coppola, Martin Scorsese and Peter Bogdanovich. On the other hand, Edward D. Wood Jr, leading the charge of the talentless, would certainly have disappeared into the annals of film history, never to be seen again, if he had not been posthumously honoured with the Medved brothers' Golden Turkey Award in 1980.

B-moves are viewed differently today and their hid-

Phyllis Kirk in *House of Wax*

den qualities are, where possible, appreciated, no longer taking a back seat to the high production values and star power of the A-movies. This turnaround isn't simply because we now allow ourselves to own up to the entertainment we get from bad taste, but is also due to the reputation the B-movie has acquired as a result of a larger postmodern transformation of aesthetic and cultural values. It was neither the studios, with their polished marketing strategies, nor the critics, with their acceptable aesthetic taste, but rather the audience and the fans who helped this often criminally neglected marginal cinema to get back on its feet.

As a rule, this re-evaluation is based on the immediate, undistorted emotion conveyed, rather than any stylistic quality of the films themselves. B-movies, even when they apparently treat serious subjects (atomic dis-

'The worst director of all time': Ed Wood and his major work...

asters, invasions, devastation), thrive on the direct effect, the cheap thrill, which could actually only be experienced by the cinema-goer in exceptional cases (like William Castle's *The Tingler* [1959], which used the 'Percepto' electrical buzzer gimmick to startle audiences). B-movies wanted to shock, to give the audience the creeps and evoke piercing screams, helpless laughter or tears. Fans were particularly taken with the way many exploitation flicks broke taboos. Full-frontal female nudity, for instance, could only be seen here, even if a film like *Mom and Dad* (1947, dir. William Beaudine) had to 'officially' deal with the birth of a child to show it. No less popular were the mad scientists and beautiful losers, freaks and aliens who populated the films, and, in a peculiar way, represented the marginal position of the B-directors in the Hollywood system. The mostly non-middle class audience could identify with these outcasts. Simple people with a desire for entertainment, enjoyment and distraction from everyday life crowded into drive-ins and downtown theatres.

B-movies also supplied budding directors with examples they could learn from — a guide to what was good as well as bad. The B-movies were a model of the dos and don'ts of film production, and a whole generation of today's film-makers grew up watching them. There are few Hollywood directors as profoundly influenced by the aesthetic of the B-movie as Tim Burton, however. In all of his films he has expressed his passionate admiration for the cheap productions he saw in his youth, even making a cinematic monument to one of the lonely heroes of that era, Edward D. Wood Jr. Tending toward the spectacular and the sensational, B-movies brought out a trend in mainstream cinema: the return to the 'cinema of attractions', to simple visual values and excessively extravagant special effects only flimsily held together by a makeshift plot structure.

Mainstream film-makers are reminded of the early days of moving pictures projected at the funfair for sheer wonder and entertainment.

Beetlejuice — The Exorcism of Holy Horror

The camera sweeps over idyllic woods and valleys, past a picturesque village with a church tower and a well, and on towards a whitewashed house with soaring Victorian gables. This outpost of paradise is called Winter River, rural Connecticut. Suddenly, a giant insect crawls over the roof of the building and is waved away by an even more enormous hand — and then we see Adam Maitland (Alec Baldwin) bending over his miniature model of the surrounding countryside, working on a few small buildings. He is gradually making a replica of the entire valley. The Maitlands' real house is a sought-after property, though, and before the sun is over the yard-arm an estate agent friend is begging the couple to accept an offer. But they decline, as they are about to begin their vacation and want to spend it at home rather than somewhere in the Pacific. A little while later, on the way back from a drive into the local town in their Volvo, a dog runs out in front of the car. Barbara Maitland (Geena Davis) swerves, and the car crashes right into a covered bridge over a river, goes through its side wall and comes to a standstill with

the front hanging dangerously over the abyss. The lucky dog is now see-sawing up and down on the other end of a pivotal floorboard — and as he jumps off and runs away, the car plunges into the deep water.

Soaking wet, the couple return home. Somehow, everything seems different, imperceptibly transformed. A cuckoo clock shows six o'clock and yet it only sounds

Poltergeist (Heather O'Rourke), *The Evil Dead* (Ellen Sandweiss), *Ghostbusters* (Sigourney Weaver, Bill Murray)

three times. As they warm themselves in front of the fire, Barbara's hands burst into flames, and her image is no longer reflected in mirrors. Finding a copy of the *Handbook for the Recently Deceased*, they begin to suspect that they are in fact no longer alive. They hit a further problem when their peace is disturbed by the arrival of a pushy yuppie family from New York City and their sulky teenage daughter, Lydia (Winona Ryder).

So begins Tim Burton's first venture into the terrain of comic horror. What he contrives to produce in *Beetlejuice* is an exorcism of the horror genre. Black comedy is used to turn everything on its head, upside down and around about. Where there was genuine horror, there will be spooky fun. Situated somewhere between fantasy, horror and comedy, *Beetlejuice* makes generous use of the many conventions these different traditions offer. Burton plays with the genre set pieces with a touch of irony, in a manner as eccentric as it is uninhibited. In particular, this film is based on a well-worn horror sub-genre, the haunted house movie. Burton makes full use of relevant cinematic examples; serious ones, such as *Poltergeist* (1982, dir. Tobe Hooper) or *The Evil Dead* (1983, dir. Sam Raimi), as well as comic ones like *Ghostbusters* (1984, dir. Ivan Reitman). What he produced is in fact not quite a horror-comedy, but rather an inversion of the typical horror scenario which makes its many clichés and stereotypes especially obvious. This is already apparent in the opening scenes, where it isn't people who are being disturbed by the presence of

ghosts, but ghosts disturbed by the presence of people.

The Maitlands soon discover that they have access to the Other Side, a colourful realm inhabited by ghosts and spirits. Football players, pale as death and much the worse for wear after a recent plane crash, look confusedly for the men's toilet as well as an explanation for their situation. Helpful support is provided at the reception desk, where Juno (Sylvia Sidney) is as familiar with the problems of the newly dead as she is bored by them. She knows, of course, that the living constitute the greatest difficulty for a dead person. When the Maitlands explain that they want to drive the unwanted guests out of their house, but they don't know how, Juno advises them to use the only tried and tested means available to ghosts and carry out a haunting.

However, as the Maitlands soon realise, at first the living barely notice them at all. Only the melancholic

Confused: Adam and Barbara Maitland (Alec Baldwin, Geena Davis)

Mild horror: Barbara Maitland pulling a few faces

daughter, Lydia ('My whole life is a dark room'), is sensitive enough to get wind of their presence, but she is unperturbed by the mostly silly disguises and pathetic noises the dead couple come up with. Her parents are just as unruffled when they finally catch on. Delia and Charles Deetz (Catherine O'Hara and Jeffrey Jones) actually consider setting up a business to exploit the unhappy poltergeists. They invite their jaded New York friends to the haunted house and plan to transform the secluded village into a ghost town, a commercial centre for the paranormal.

Gradually, the Maitlands improve their act, slipping into designer sheets, trying out grotesque grimaces in front of the mirror and rolling their eyes (as they hold them in their hands). In their hour of greatest need they appeal to the 'bio-exorcist', Betelgeuse, who promises to cast out the living, or so his television advertisement claims. Betelgeuse (Michael Keaton), a spirit with a dubious reputation, was once Juno's assistant, till he fell out of favour and went freelance. Constantly scratching his crotch and chasing every skirt he sees, this particularly horny devil takes up residence in Adam Maitland's model village and waits in the miniature cemetery for the Maitlands to say his name three times before he can rise up like a genie from a bottle.

Michael Keaton acts the part of the fiend with great skill and energy. Burton's first choice was actually Sammy Davis Jr, but Warners favoured Keaton. Burton, who claims not to have followed Keaton's previous career, soon came round to their

 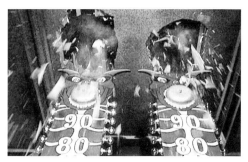

way of thinking, and especially appreciated Keaton's unique humour, which was already apparent in one of the actor's early showpieces, Ron Howard's *Night Shift* (1982). They worked together on two subsequent occasions, when Burton cast Keaton as Bruce Wayne and his alter ego in *Batman* and *Batman Returns*, but the actor never got another opportunity to let off quite as much steam as in the finale of *Beetlejuice*, with his demonstration of supernatural strength. During a séance in the

Trial of strength: Michael Keaton as Betelgeuse

The middle class family in *Hellraiser*

Deetz's house, Lydia calls out in desperation for Betelgeuse, hoping to expel her parents' cultural dilettante friends once and for all with his assistance. But Lydia finds that she cannot then get rid of her poltergeist, and only at the last minute is she able to thwart his evil intentions. Thus, the Maitlands are released from their detention in Purgatory, and eternal peace returns to the house.

Let there be fun!

Beetlejuice was an early display of Tim Burton's brilliance. At a time when other directors were starting a renaissance of 'serious' horror, Burton was attempting a parody of the same. It's no coincidence that *Beetlejuice* clearly references the film *Hellraiser* (1986), directed by British horror writer Clive Barker, although the movie had not actually been out for very long. Reacting to several years of rather camp horror-comedies, Barker, a hugely commercially successful horror novelist *a la* Stephen King, tried to rehabilitate the genre in the mid-eighties by combining elements of classic horror, mysticism and, above all, sexual perversion. *Hellraiser*, his first film as a director, was based on his own novella *The Hellbound Heart*. It was particularly influential for the modern horror film, not only because of the use of Christian symbols and iconography (the four horsemen of the apocalypse, Purgatory, the realm of Atonement), but also for bringing the associated sadomasochism out into the open. In search of the ultimate pleasure — at the point where it crosses into tortuous pain — and with the aid of a mystical puzzle box, a young man called Frank ventures into regions of a demonic world which becomes his undoing. Only when his brother, sister-in-law and niece move into the house where he died does a bloody accident unexpectedly give him a new life. His niece discovers the secret of the magic box and sends the four apocalyptic Cenobites after him ('No tears, please. It's a

Not exactly gloomy: the house in
Beetlejuice

waste of good suffering'). Finally, they catch up with Frank and kill him a second time — a thousand hooks pierce his flesh as he is tortured and literally torn to pieces. His last words are 'Jesus wept'.

In Tim Burton's *Beetlejuice* one is always close to tears — tears of laughter. Burton took out all the elements of cruelty from the *Hellraiser* model, which for its part used many genre stereotypes (the hidden entrance into a forbidden demonic world, the revenge of the spirits thereby disturbed, the mutation of the intruders into spirits themselves, and so on). Typically, there isn't a drop of blood to be seen in *Beetlejuice*, as Burton explains: 'I always had my own ideas about the way it should be — if there's darkness there should be colour and light. *Beetlejuice* was a real mix of colour and dark to me, and I wanted to temper a lot of the darker aspects and make it a bit more colourful' (*Burton on Burton*, Mark Salisbury). Thus, he romanticised the individual elements from the bottom up, enriched them with contemporary culture and made them conform to his own ideas. The result combines comedy, fantasy, horror and farce, openly borrowing from the geometrically innovative, neon-bright stylistic artifice of the eighties — the Other Side meets the here and now.

One example of how *Beetlejuice* inverts horror clichés is the treatment of the haunted house trope. The Maitland's house is a brilliant white, middle class

Winona Ryder as daughter Lydia

affair whose gables and towers are only very remotely related to the gloomy buildings immortalised as temples of terror in *Psycho* (1960, dir. Alfred Hitchcock) and *The Old Dark House* (1932, dir. James Whale), for example. One of Delia Deetz's arty New York friends, interior designer Otho (Glenn Shadix), gets rid of any remaining traces of the traditional colonial style and gives the interior a makeover in the cold New Wave fashion. The eighties are also represented by the character of Lydia, a fan of the New Romantic fashion and music. Dressed in black, wearing a veil and assorted goth jewellery, she concerns herself with demonic phenomena partly for reasons of style. Here, Burton is making a connection between a contemporary phenomenon and the dark, Gothic side of Romanticism which was the original

source of horror cinema. (It should also be said that Lydia bears a striking, and not merely physical, resemblance to Tim Burton himself, and she may be seen as another incarnation of his alter ego.)

The intermediate world of the spirits is designed as a veritable pop pandemonium, with its black and white chessboard floor and neon décor. As a contrast to this ultra-modern (as it was then) style, other rooms feature the distinctive distorted perspectives of Expressionism, with bizarre painted backdrops clearly reminiscent of *The Cabinet of Dr Caligari* (1919, dir. Robert Wiene). Drawing on a wide range of references spanning several decades of the history of film and architecture, Tim Burton operates at the forefront of contemporary culture — in the eighties, that meant a culture which lost all belief in any natural connection between signs and their meanings. The motto was 'anything goes' and, compared with his later films, when Burton worked more concertedly on getting his homages and references to make sense, *Beetlejuice* is a virtuoso exercise in deconstruction. Nothing is sacred in this comic haunted house.

In the waiting room of the underworld, a scene owing more to farce than horror, several eccentric characters hang around — a man who choked to death on a chicken bone; the remains of someone who died in bed, still puffing away on a cigarette; a girl sawn in two who requires two chairs to sit down (one for her upper half and one for her lower half). Tim Burton consciously parodies another horror theme here — the violent death. Cameraman Thomas Ackerman described this intermediate world as follows: 'If you imagine Purgatory as an eternal sojourn in an office where you apply for an extension of your driving licence, you'll get an idea of what we wanted. It wasn't to be scary except in an unusual way. The main afterlife set is a huge secretary's office with a row of desks as far as you can see, surrounded by a sea of computer paper... This is where the recently deceased are assigned a task in order to resolve that which was left unresolved at the time of their passing' (*American Cinematographer*, 4/1998). This scenario of atonement and unfinished business, which often inspired horror characters to carry out drastic acts, becomes utterly mundane in *Beetlejuice*.

Burton quite deliberately sets out to create this cheap, cartoon impression, allowing the Maitlands to enter the underworld in an absurdly simple manner by drawing the outline of a door on the wall with chalk. However, as soon as the couple set foot outside their own front door proper they find themselves in a surrealist landscape worthy of Salvador Dali, with an azure blue sky hanging over bizarre desert vegetation and giant worms ploughing through the sand. Greetings from David Lynch's *Dune* (1984)! Lynch, for his part, borrowed a great deal from surrealist cinema — *Blue Velvet* (1986), for example, is indebted to Luis Buñuel's *Un Chien Andalou* (1928). In Buñuel's film, a man stares aghast at a hole in his ant-covered hand; in Lynch's film, Jeffrey Beaumont (Kyle MacLachlan) finds an ear in a meadow that's crawling with ants. Such symbols of disgust have always provided inspiration for horror films. Clive Barker, for example, fixated on any kind of imagery which audiences would find repulsive — insects nesting in decaying corpses, dripping slime, and a good deal of dark red blood — culturally loaded semiotic material with a shock effect that could never be blatant enough.

Tim Burton is particularly good at ironic variations on such chains of recognisable symbols, which he skilfully adds to. Betelgeuse's appearance wasn't so much fearsome as grotesque and macabre (Ve Neill, Steve LaPorte and Robert Short won an Oscar for their character make-up). 'We wanted Michael [Keaton] to look like he'd crawled out from under a rock,' Burton explained (*Burton on Burton*, Mark Salisbury). Keaton was well able to carry through the character's trademark hyperactivity, dining on insects and cockroaches from his trouser pockets, which he consumes with obvious pleasure, farting loudly in the process. When he is about to feast on a fly, it squeals a high-pitched 'Help me!' like the cloned scientist Delambre in *The Fly* (1958, dir. Kurt Neumann). There is no doubt about it — Betelgeuse represents the most ridiculous horror character of all time and the movie cleverly parodies fiendish

Cheesy: the gateway to Hell

monsters everywhere. This is, perhaps, the exorcism of the devil from the horror film.

'It's just something I do'

The original idea for *Beetlejuice* goes back to David Geffen, a film producer and record label owner (artists he has worked with include Aerosmith, Guns 'N' Roses and Cher), and one of the team behind the successful genre outing *Little Shop of Horrors* (1986, dir. Frank Oz). Geffen offered Michael Mc-Dowell's screenplay to Tim Burton, who was considered bizarre but potentially bankable after the success of *Pee-wee's Big Adventure*. According to Burton, it was more of an amorphous 'stream of consciousness' than a watertight script and he made sure that his friend, scriptwriter Warren Skaaren, had a hand in the alterations. The screenplay went through several drafts until it displayed the requisite Burton touch.

Tim Burton has always liked to claim that he approaches his work in a purely intuitive fashion, saying, 'I never think about it, it's just something I do' (*Burton on Burton*, Mark Salisbury). The precision and accuracy with which he operates, however, call this into question. The systematic deconstruction of the demonic, mythological and religious paraphernalia of the horror films referred to in *Beetlejuice* seems too deliberate to be purely a matter of instinct. He sails around obvious narrative cliff-hangers with great care, avoiding the traditional climactic scenes — his fundamental principle here is the anti-climax, alien by nature to all true horror films. In *Beetlejuice* (as in Burton's other films), when the aesthetic and semantic registers no longer synchronise and familiar symbols have lost their traditional meanings, it's a deliberate result of the semiotic spectacle Burton stages. He presents us with a circus of signs, scenarios and stock themes robbed of their original context and meaning; a noisy, colourful, disorientating show true to the B-movie tradition.

Batman – Economics and Subversion

It may seem far-fetched to compare a mega-production like *Batman* with a $50,000 B-movie, but there is a common thread, namely the paramount importance of economic success — albeit at opposite ends of the scale. Even B-movies employed a promotional campaign to improve their uncertain prospects. A marketing executive from Roger Corman's production company in New York estimated that the first impression a film makes on its potential audience is about seventy per cent dependent on its title and advertising campaign. Lurid titles such as Herschell Gordon Lewis' *The Gore Gore Girls* (1972) and incendiary poster slogans like 'Women so hot with desire they melt the chains that enslave them' for Jack Hill's *The Big Bird Cage* (1972) give an insight into the vivid imaginations of the exploitation movie-makers.

A similarly targeted strategy was undertaken for 1989's *Batman*, launched by an advertising campaign of an unparalleled scale. It was deemed an absolute necessity, as success was by no means guaranteed throughout the complicated development stage. This particular incarnation of the *Batman* myth began life in 1979 when two scriptwriters, Michael Uslan and Ben Melniker, acquired the film rights to the *Batman* material and offered them to Hollywood producer Peter Guber. At the time, Guber was working for the mini-major studio Casablanca, which was taken over the following year by Polygram. He was enthusiastic about the idea of giving Batman back his darker side, which had been an integral part of the character in the original comics by Bob Kane. After negotiations over several years, during which Peter Guber teamed up

Batman swoops into the world: the first comic, 1939

with Jon Peters and moved to Warner Bros, as well as countless draft scripts offered to well-known directors, including Joe Dante and Ivan Reitman, there was still no sign whatsoever of a definite start date for production. Serious discussions didn't get under way until 1986, quickly involving up-and-coming young director Tim Burton. Warner was not bound to honour old arrangements, and Uslan and Melniker only learned from the newspapers that production had actually begun. They then contacted Warner Bros, who gave them the choice of signing a supplementary contract or not being involved in the film at all. 'On 8 September, 1988, they signed a new contract which gave them nominal credit as executive producers, stripped them of creative involvement and consulting rights, and granted them thirteen percent of net profits. As all but the rankest amateurs in Hollywood know, net points are generally worthless,' explain Nancy Griffin and Kim Masters in their book *Hit and Run: How Jon Peters and Peter Guber took Sony for a Ride in Hollywood.* Uslan and Melniker chose to take the screen credit, each earning $300,000. Although the total proceeds of the film are estimated at over two billion dollars, Griffin and Masters say they didn't make any further profit from it: 'According to Warner Bros, *Batman* is still in the red.'

It was only after the relatively big success of *Beetlejuice* (gross proceeds estimated at eighty million dollars) that Tim Burton was finally signed up to direct *Batman.* Warner executives waited to see the box office takings of his previous film; after all, they didn't want to back the wrong horse. Together with his writer, Sam Hamm, Burton presented Warner with a thirty-page treatment based on the successful *Batman*

adaptations of comics writer/artist Frank Miller, which managed to convince the decision-makers, despite its rather dark, downbeat atmosphere. Experienced scriptwriters Charles McKeown and (again at Burton's express wish) Warren Skaaren continued to make daily alterations even during shooting. Warner Communications Inc was at the time involved in a merger with media giant Time, and *Batman* was supposed to provide the necessary capital. The result was a publicity strategy the like of which had never been seen before.

'*Batman* took the United States by storm in the spring and summer of 1989. T-shirts, posters, keychains, jewellery, buttons, books, watches, magazines, trading cards, audiotaped books, videogames, records, cups and numerous other items flooded malls across the United States with images of Batman, his new logo and his old enemy the Joker. Presaged by a much pirated trailer, *Batman* the film drew unprecedented crowds to theatre chains, of which the two largest (United Artists Theatre Circuits and American Multi-Cinema) distributed four to five million brochures for mail order Bat-materials. *Batman*'s première on the big screen was matched by appearances

Batman chewing gum wrapper: merchandising circa 1966

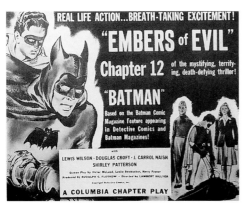

Forerunners: posters for the *Batman* serials of the 1940s

on the small screen. Film clips were packaged as advertisements and free promotional materials for the interview and movie review circuits on both broadcast and cable television; Prince's 'Batdance' video played in heavy rotation on MTV. Over radio, 'Batdance' and other cuts from Prince's *Batman* album got strong play on rock stations and "crossed over" for similarly strong play on black radio stations. Subsequently, retail outlets filled with Bat-costumes and Joker make-up kits for Halloween; Ertl Batmobiles and ToyBiz Batcaves and Batwings were were being deployed for Christmas shoppers. In the speciality stores serving comics fandom, the *Advance Comics Special Batlist* offered 214 items ranging from $576 to $2 in price. And in grocery stores, special Bat-displays offered children a choice between *Batman* colouring books, *Batman* trace-and-colour books and *Batman* magic plates' (*The Many Lives of the Batman*, ed. Roberta E. Pearson, William Uricchio).

This is how Eileen R. Meehan described an advertising campaign bigger than any that had been seen before, even in the USA. Particularly memorable was the movie poster image — the Batlogo, the black shape of a bat in a yellow oval in front of a solid black background. Under the logo, all that was printed was the release date; no film title, no actors' names, no director's name.

Warner had secured the film rights and the copyright to the logo long before the film came out — DC Comics, publishers of the original Bob Kane strips, has been part of Warner Communications Inc since 1971. The entire *Batman* range was contained under the roof of the media conglomerate, whose diversified interests even then ensured multiple profit opportunities. Synergistic activities in the video and television business, merchandising and the many other in-house products, including Prince's hit album, made it possible for the marketing campaign to cover a huge area. The watchword of the time was cross-promotion, meaning that products were used to advertise and sell each other.

In order to be sure that the main feature — the movie — would also be well-received by consumers, Warner carried out market research of the comics market, along with the famous test screenings. The studio was sure of the average fan — twenty years old, male and willing to spend ten dollars a week on the comics, but they also hoped to attract other age groups, including the older reader of traditional comics, by the sale of toy figures in both the original Bob Kane style and the newer movie design by Anton Furst. The casting of actors associated with totally different genres and characters was intended to appeal to different demographic profiles, and Prince had the job of bringing in the black audience. And finally, Tim Burton, known for his extensive range of quotations from and references to earlier films and eras, also promised to appeal to earlier generations of fans still familiar with the *Batman* saga of the forties film serial or the camp television series.

A late summer release date was also part of this strategic fine tuning. *Batman* didn't take over the run-up to the summer season, as a film of this scale normally would — that honour was left to *Indiana Jones and the Last Crusade* (1989, dir. Steven Spielberg).

Burt Ward as Robin and Adam West as Batman in the 1960s' television series

Previews in several cities ensured the requisite word-of-mouth build-up and augmented the sense of an event which surrounded the film. The film was an absolute must — not to see it virtually made one a social pariah.

All the effort and expense paid dividends, as is well documented. *Batman* still stands as one of the most profitable projects in film history, with box office takings in the US alone estimated at $250 million; total proceeds reportedly amounted to a half a billion dollars, not including the video and television sales or merchandising. For a film which cost a mere fifty million dollars, this was a phenomenal success. Nobody had reckoned with this, least of all the director: 'The first time you direct a film of this proportion is somehow surreal' (*Burton on Burton*, Mark Salisbury).

The world makes sense if you force it to

Batman is pure style, or, at least, it demonstrates a strong drive for style, as demonstrated in Anton Furst's Oscar-winning production design. Huge backdrops almost thirty metres high were erected to original scale over five months in Pinewood Studios, near London, in order to create Gotham City, described 'as if hell had erupted through the pavement and kept on growing' (*Cinefex* 2/1990). Models, miniatures and drawings were only used for buildings and objects more than fifty feet high. Anton Furst set great store by mixing different styles — brownstone architecture, elements of modernism, futurism, Gothic symbols and even fascist monumental pomp. Furst wanted to create coherence from the diversity, a stylistic pastiche which would overwhelm the spectator with its sheer size. 'The most important thing was that we find a feel for the city which was neither futuristic nor historical. We wanted it to be as timeless as possible, even though — since we were drawing from the original DC comic strip for inspiration — there was bound to be a certain forties feeling to it,' he explained (*Cinefex* 2/1990).

Many critics were enthusiastic about the dramatic visual impression created by Gotham City and considered the set design to be the real star of the film, with its overwhelming mix of influences, from Expressionist to Aztec. When Roger Ebert in the *Chicago Sun-Times* described 'a triumph of design over the story and of style over substance,' complaining of a lack of tension and internal interest, he emphasised both the main focus of this 'Grand Guignol opera' (*Premiere*, 7/1989) and its greatest weakness. The entire set design represents a society in decline, an apocalyptic vision of civilisation to some extent modelled on the totalitarian underworld of Fritz Lang's *Metropolis* (1926) and the futuristic city state designed by Syd Mead in *Blade Runner*.

Furst's Gotham City is a giant Moloch, with skyscrapers shooting hundreds of metres into the sky; barely any daylight penetrates down to the streets below. Rubbish is strewn around the streets and most of the scenes take place in semi-darkness or at night. Administrative corruption, political brutalisation and social demoralisation are the order of the day in a city ruled over by an unscrupulous industrialist by the name of Carl Grissom (Jack Palance).

The story begins in a sea of houses as a couple with a child make their way through one of the overcrowded streets. They are unfamiliar with the area and have lost their way. Turning into a back

A mixture of styles: Gotham City design

The beginning: Gotham City as Moloch

alley they are attacked by gangsters and threatened with a pistol, when out of the air swoops Batman (Michael Keaton), who watched the attack from a rooftop and puts the robbers to flight. The police arrive, and can only speculate as to who or what rushed to the couple's aid, and whether it's a friend or foe. This constitutes an introductory scene, mirroring the story of how Bruce Wayne's alter ego Batman was born. When he was a child, Bruce Wayne's parents lost their lives in a similar incident. A small-time crook by the name of Jack Napier (Jack Nicholson) was involved back then, and he now becomes Batman's nemesis — the Joker.

It was part of Tim Burton's declared intention to provide the characters with a certain amount of ambivalence, though he sometimes only manages to do this in outline. The most convincing scene in this respect is the birth of the Joker. As revenge for Napier's affair with Carl Grissom's lover, fashion victim Alicia (Jerry Hall), Grissom sends Napier into an ambush which leads to a confrontation between Napier and Batman in the Axis Chemicals factory. Napier ends up dangling over a steaming vat of green chemicals, clutching Batman's hand, and it's impossible to say whether Batman deliberately lets him fall. After considerable cosmetic surgery, Napier, believed dead, rises again, his face permanently contorted into a grin framed by ashen skin and green hair. After the key scene explaining the birth of the Batman character, the Joker's unique origin makes clear how inherently responsible Batman and the

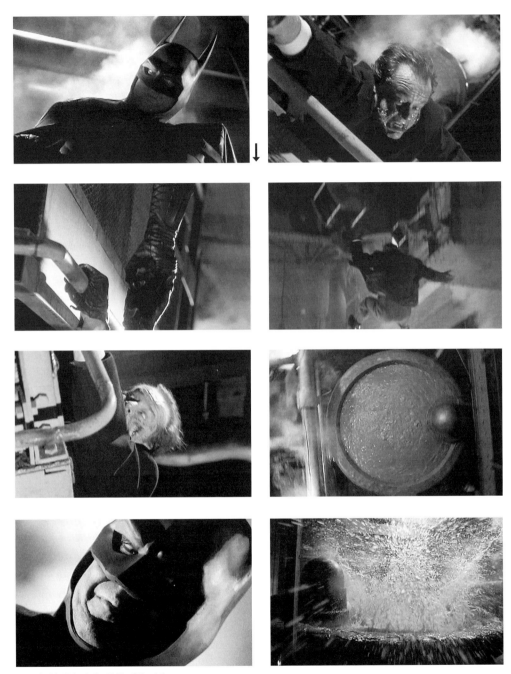

Inextricably linked: the birth of the Joker

Comic aesthetics: the Batwing as Batlogo

Joker are for the existence of the other.

After the Joker has had his revenge on Grissom by killing him, he wants to get his own back on Batman and is not pleased that his arch-enemy has become headline news: 'Can somebody tell me what kind of a world we live in where a man dressed up as a bat gets all my press?' In the meantime, journalist Alexander Knox (Robert Wuhl) and photographer Vicki Vale (Kim Basinger) have started following the Batman story. At an exclusive social gathering in Wayne Manor, host Bruce Wayne and the good-looking photographer get to know each other better and later become intimate. As a confirmed bachelor, however, Wayne — unlike his alter ego, Batman — shies away from responsibility and their relationship appears to be going nowhere due to his inability to make up his mind. In the meantime, the Joker is taking decisive steps to seize control of Gotham City. He introduces a poison into a range of cosmetic products which ensures its users die with a painful smile on their lips. Burton's characteristic sense of humour is evident in the scene showing television presenters who have had to do without make-up, and consequently look spotty and pale.

A further highpoint is the scene in the Flugelheim Museum where the Joker uses a pretext to meet Vicki Vale. It's abundantly clear that the intentions of the 'first fully-functional homicidal artist' are not the purest. He can no longer stand beauty and shows himself to be a real iconoclast, offhandedly painting over a

Renoir and a De Chirico. A wall in an Edward Hopper painting is left with the graffiti 'Joker was here!' Only a painting by Francis Bacon, showing old, wrinkled flesh, is left unscathed.

The Joker's clown-like costume, which stands out among the otherwise restrained colours of the film, is intended to distract from his real, evil intentions. Poisonous gas streams out of enormous balloons at a parade advertised to the masses on television with the promise of several million dollars to be distributed among them. There follows a duel between the Joker and Batman, during which it only takes one shot from the Joker's gun to ward off an air attack from the Batwing. The aesthetic of comics and B-movies comes to the fore here, emphasised by the décor. During his descent into the city, Batman races along the painted canyons of the streets and then takes off again into the sky, breaking through a bank of cloud to position the Batwing in front of the yellow moon, thereby creating the silhouette of the Batlogo — a nice gag and also a reference to the colourful sixties *Batman* television series.

Conversely, one can also appreciate the sparse scenery found in other parts of the film, such as the forest Batman roars through in the Batmobile on the way to the Batcave, which looks like a quick cartoon drawing. Or the Joker's final defeat, which takes place in time-honoured comic fashion — he is hurled from the tower of Gotham cathedral into the abyss with a stone gargoyle at his feet, making

Comic aesthetics (II): the Joker after his fall

From the first *Batman* comic, 1939

a deep, Joker-shaped crater in the ground where he lands, just like a cartoon character. Despite the film's seriously high production values, the style is still occasionally allowed to tend towards the cheap and cartoony.

The myth and legend of Batman

Tim Burton expressed his dissatisfaction with his first Batman film on several occasions: 'Torture — the worst period of my life' (*Hit and Run*, Nancy Griffin, Kim Masters). The production conditions in particular were far from ideal. Casting decisions were changed without warning, and whole scenes were turned upside down from one day to the next. 'We were shooting a scene leading up to the bell tower and Jack's walking up the steps, but we didn't know why. He said to me that day. "Why am I going up the steps?" And I said, "I don't know, we'll talk about it when you get up the top"' (*Burton on Burton*, Mark Salisbury). This illustrates the extent to which Burton had lost control, but it is also an indication of his well-known weakness as a director — the flow of the narrative is uneven at several points (only partly a conscious tribute to the comicbook style), the balance of the characters doesn't quite work (Nicholson steals the show from Keaton) and, furthermore, the editing is careless and the soundtrack very fragmented.

Tim Burton tried to stay as faithful as possible to Bob Kane's Batman character first presented in the American comicbook series *Detective Comics* (no 27) in May 1939. From 1940, stories about the 'Dark Knight' filled their own volume, resulting in a popularity which the character has never lost. An

American myth had been born whose different incarnations closely reflected the socio-cultural situation in America at any given time. While the ambiguous, justice fanatic Batman presented in the Kane comics was as appropriate for the years after the Great Depression as the film noir which developed around the same time, there is a distinct feeling of propaganda to the first film serial which Columbia started in 1943, corresponding to the involvement of the USA in the Second World War. In 1949, the second series invoked the paranoia of the Cold War and at the same time reminded audiences of their fear of the axis powers; there was talk of 'axis criminals', a term echoed in Burton's film in the name of Grissom's factory — Axis Chemicals.

Stylistically, the film serial, shot in brilliant sunlight, has as little to do with Burton's dark work as the up-beat

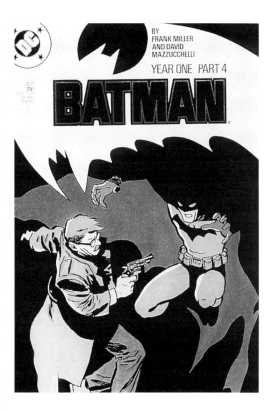

Batman in the eighties: *Year One*

comics of the fifties, the years of America's economic miracle. When, in 1954, the Comics Code Authority was set up, as a result of pressure from the public, to see that representations of the family, public order and violence were in accordance with contemporary moral standards, this spelled the end of any kind of ambivalence in the vigilante's saga. The *Batman* television series launched by ABC on 12 January 1966 quickly became a hit, with such recognisable faces as Tallulah Bankhead, Zsa Zsa Gabor and Joan Collins scrambling for parts. The series had hardly anything in common with the original concept of the character, and the real, hard-boiled Batman fans were unimpressed. Batman, the dark avenger, was no longer a *bad man*, driven by his mission, but rather a naïve pop hero in a flashy costume who didn't know what was happening himself most of the time. It was only when comics creators Dennis O'Neil, Neal Adams, Frank Miller and Alan Moore began to look again at the original and relate it to the contemporary climate — O'Neil and Adams creating a social realism typical of the seventies; Miller and Moore invoking visions of urban apocalypse in the eighties. In particular, the Miller title *Batman: Year One*, explaining the back story behind Bruce Wayne's trauma, is one of the most visually interesting.

Just as B-movies took up influential social trends — like the fifties atom bomb paranoia — Tim Burton set *Batman* against the background of the social erosion in America of the end of the eighties and thereby brought the comic strip bang up to date. The headlines of the time were full of crime, corruption, scandals and businessmen interfering in the political decision-making process. Even the psychic make-up of the hero was influenced by contemporary discussions about multiple personality disorder, a subject taken up again even more explicitly in the sequel *Batman Returns*. Of course, that's not to say that Burton owed much to social realism — the film is much too conscious of the history of the Batman legend for that, and is stylistically situated in a temporal nirvana which does not allow any direct parallels with the here and now. However, in *Batman,* Burton made his most political film — the smash hit breakthrough of subversion into mass culture, into mainstream cinema, which usually claims to cater to the position of the moral majority, refusing dissident voices success. Even if traditional comic fans went to the barricades and saw the *Batman* project as a capitulation to commerce, the mere fact that this film shows a schizophrenic becoming a cult toy figure must be seen as something of a *coup*.

Ed Wood — No American Dream!

'Greetings, my friends. You are interested in the unknown, the mysterious, the unexplainable... that is why you are here. So now, for the first time, we are giving you all the evidence, based only on the secret testimony of the miserable souls who survived the terrifying ordeal. Can your hearts stand the shocking facts of the true story of Edward D. Wood Jr?'

Ed Wood begins with these words, spoken in the authoritative tones of Criswell, a popular television medium in the fifties. The film recreates episodes from the life of B-movie icon Wood, said to be 'the worst director of all time'. Critical appraisals notwithstanding, the recent revival of interest in the popular culture of the fifties and sixties has led to Ed Wood's *oeuvre* being properly appreciated at last. Interest (and not just from Tim Burton) in this particular period has been inspired by the eccentricity and individualism of the directors then working in the low-budget, off-beat margins of Hollywood. Tim Burton and scriptwriters Scott Alexander and Larry Karaszewski stayed broadly true to the facts remembered and recorded as oral history

in Rudolph Grey's *Nightmare of Ecstasy: The Life and Art of Edward D. Wood, Jr* (Feral House), in which long-standing friends and colleagues give an account of their time with Ed Wood. Burton does depart from the facts, occasionally; in his biopic, he takes the liberty of painting a more optimistic portrait than Grey's book — quite the opposite of the tragic course of Wood's real life.

One must remember to visualise trash legend Ed Wood as an optimist bursting with relentless ambition but totally lacking in talent; an absolute wannabe who modelled himself extravagantly on Orson Welles.

During his lifetime, Wood didn't even manage to achieve success with his B-movies. His films are crude mixtures of bad scenes and stock footage whose origin and semantic meaning seem to be the director's best-kept secrets. Cheap tricks and special effects were part of Wood's repertoire, but, contrary to cinematic folk-lore, he didn't actually use Cadillac hubcaps as flying saucers. Nowadays, what seems most disturbing about his films are the long monologues used to explain the setting and the plot to his audience, torrents of words about technical details which seem to go on for ever. Wood, a loser in every way, spent his life chasing his dream of money and recognition. He lived his last few years in poverty, writing 'penny dreadfuls' and making soft porn, and died an alcoholic in 1978.

It took Tim Burton to work the miracle of turning base material into gold, as it were. Compared with Wood's original films, which can be painful to sit through, Burton's *Ed Wood* is elegant and amusing in equal parts. Of course, this has a lot to do with Burton breaking off the story of Wood's life at the point where he had reached his creative zenith with *Plan 9 from Outer Space* in 1959. As Wood himself foretold, 'This is the one they'll remember me for.' Success is always relative, and Ed Wood had nothing to be ashamed of when it came to productivity, releasing a total of thirty films, developing numerous unrealised projects and writing even more trashy novels with promising titles like *Death of a Transvestite — Let Me Die in Drag* (1967), *The Sexecutives* (1968) and *TV Lust* (1977). During his final decade he concentrated almost exclusively on sexploitation.

This overtly sexual subject matter isn't characteris-tic of the Ed Wood films still around today — book publishing was more liberal than the movies in those days. However, the representation of sexuality could be legitimised by apparently didactic intentions. From time to time, naked facts could be shown under the cover of half-serious sexual education and well-mean-ing advice. In one of Wood's early films, *Glen or*

Glenda (1953, aka *I Led 2 Lives/I Changed My Sex/He or She?*), a grand appeal for reason and understanding, the hero is a man who likes to wear women's clothes. He has to battle with the problems caused by his behaviour, and can't bring himself to reveal his dubious secret to his girlfriend. In one scene, the collapse of the boundaries between the sexes is visually represented by a male Y-chromosome in the form of a tree falling on a woman. Symbolism to knock you flat! (incidentally, *Glen or Glenda* is one of David Lynch's favourite movies.)

During *Glen or Glenda*, Ed Wood was personally active on the emancipation front as usual — right at the front, playing the eponymous transvestite under the pseudonym Daniel Davis. Even while shooting, Wood liked to wear drag, and in Tim Burton's film his

Ed Wood (Johnny Depp) with his wife Kathy O'Hara (Patricia Arquette)

Crummy scenery, archive footage, amateurish special effects: *Plan 9 from Outer Space*

↓

It's just not you!: Ed Wood, Dolores Fuller (Sarah Jessica Parker)

clothes fetish and taste for angora play an important role. The B-movie-maker, with all his eccentricities, is sensitively played by Johnny Depp. As Edward Scissorhands, Depp had already demonstrated an affinity with Burton's outsider figures, an empathy which also comes through in his other film roles — *What's Eating Gilbert Grape* (1993, dir. Lasse Hallström), for example, where he plays a son collapsing under the weight of responsibility for his family; or *Dead Man* (1996, dir. Jim Jarmusch), playing William Blake setting out from Puritanical Cleveland for the Wild West in search of work. In *Ed Wood*, Depp becomes the eccentric filmmaker whose relationship with Dolores Fuller, the star of Wood's early projects, is punctuated by the occasional row about who gets to wear the angora. Depp plays this enthusiastic no-talent with the utmost dedication.

How can any race be so stupid?

When the young Ed Wood reads of the Christine Jorgensen story (headline: 'Ex-GI turned Glamour Girl') in *Variety* he immediately contacts Georgie Weiss (Mike Starr), a producer for down-market Screen Classics who also holds the rights to the story. Ed considers himself to be absolutely the right man for the cross-dresser material — after all, during the Second World War he served in the American army wearing women's underclothes beneath his uniform. The burly producer cannot quite follow his arguments, but in the end he gives his consent. 'Is there a script?' Ed asks him. 'Fuck, no! But there's a poster.' Just prior to this, Wood had come across reclusive actor Bela Lugosi, the Universal horror star famous for the 1931 *Dracula*, outside a funeral parlour.

This has-been star, whose fame had long faded by the fifties, still made a great impression on the real Ed Wood, and they became close friends up to Lugosi's death. Wood made Lugosi a kind of master of ceremonies in *Glen or Glenda*, and in Burton's film his crude lines are brilliantly intoned by Martin Landau: 'Bevare, bevare — bevare of the big grrreen drrragon that sits on your doorsteps!'

In Lugosi, Wood got himself not only a star but also a morphine addict. Only a syringe and a stiff drink were capable of bringing the old Hungarian to life, but everything could go like clockwork — he successfully wrestled the giant octopus in *Bride of the Monster* (1955), for instance, manipulating the tentacles himself, as well as filming scenes for *Plan 9 from Outer Space*. Lugosi died during the shooting of *Plan 9* and his friend, chiropractor Dr Tom Mason (Ned Bellamy), jumped in at short notice to replace him, holding his arm in front of his face and wearing a toupee so nobody would notice the difference. Lugosi, stuck with his Dracula image to the bitter end of his career, made himself the talk of the town one last time when he voluntarily registered with the California State Hospital for treatment for his drug addiction shortly before his death, and the popular press had a field day.

Bela Lugosi (Martin Landau) fighting with the octopus

Wood's first long-term partner, Dolores Fuller (Sarah Jessica Parker), was deeply resentful of both his transvestism and his friends: 'You're surrounding your-self with a bunch of weirdos.' And, as Burton's biopic amply demonstrates, those who gathered around the would-be director were not always so talented them-selves. Cameraman William C. Thompson (Norman Alden), afflicted with red-green colour-blindness; Swedish wrestler Tor Johnson (George 'The Animal' Steele) covering all the monster parts; Criswell (Jeffrey Jones), who had, without any qualification for the part except a certain gravitas, managed to become a televi-sion prophet predicting miracles as well as the end of the world on prime-time television; and permanently black-clad Vampira (Lisa Marie), known in everyday life as actress Maila Nurmi, who hosted her own horror show on KABC in the early fifties and later ran a mail order company specialising in copies of gravestones of the famous. The fact that their fortunes were tied, for better or worse, to the success of the films bound the lit-tle group more closely together. As Ed Wood was work-ing without the backing of a Hollywood studio, he had to go on the offensive in search of contacts and finan-ciers, once promising a Baptist community in Beverly Hills that he would produce a series of Bible films with the 'inevitable profits' which would accrue from *Plan 9 from Outer Space*. What was truly inevitable, however, was the prompt failure of the movie, also eminently apparent to the creditors.

In a scene in which Depp's Ed, once again directing in drag, finds himself the butt of a joke on account of his get-up, he furiously throws in the towel, storms out of the rented studio, hails a taxi and drives to a bar where he knocks back a whiskey. The barman is played by Conrad Brooks, an actor who was one of the policemen in the original *Plan 9*. And who should happen to be in a corner of the same bar but Orson Welles (Vincent D'Onofrio), Ed's great hero, from whom he gets some welcome moral support: 'Visions are worth fighting for.

Why waste your time making other people's dreams?' This motto could apply to Wood's entire *oeuvre*, which it would be no exaggeration to describe as entirely his own work. Ed Wood was undoubtedly a genuine *auteur*, egocentric through and through — a *writer-producer-actor-director*! Wood's great professional weakness was the fact that he needed to maintain a personal connection to his material, in B-movies where individuality tended to be a disadvantage, rather than conforming to the rigorous formulae of the genre pictures. He probably would have felt more at home among avant-garde artists in Paris of the twenties or in the heterogeneous subculture of the sixties, which make the Wood clique look like a shabby caricature.

Ed's Tinseltown — Tim's Hollywood

Burton illustrated the distance, both literal and metaphorical, between Ed Wood and the dream factory right at the beginning of the film, as the camera pulls back from the Hollywood sign on the hillside, along the valley floor and over the cityscape until it stops in front of a shabby theatre on the edge of town where the première of Wood's first play is taking place. Ed Wood was never able to walk back along the long path so smoothly followed by the camera — and by Tim Burton himself. He remained firmly behind the fence, peeking over at the glittering world below him. Nevertheless, his lack of success didn't affect his confidence, if one doesn't take into account his later alcoholism. 'I was fascinated by his biz-

Shooting *Plan 9 from Outer Space*

Burton's Ed Wood films and watches Bela Lugosi's final scenes...

arrely perverted optimism,' Tim Burton explains, 'because that was something I had also started out with and which then somehow wore off. Ed Wood had revitalised me. I like this duality in the character, like in *Batman*, the idea of hiding something which is inside one' (*Film Comment*, 11-12, 1994).

Thus, the film also highlights the ultimate self-denial characterising the life of Ed Wood, who could only live out his transvestism through his creative activities (or the illusory world of the studios and friends he considered as such) and vice versa. It was a kind of self-therapy hiding a glaring dissociation; the open denial of society's concept of normality outside and in front of its very gates. In Burton's film, this seems less complicated. It's almost as if the halo he places over Wood continues to shine despite Wood's lack of success, and the self-destructiveness barely evident in the movie. Ed Wood is a perfect addition to Burton's gallery of outsider-heroes and Burton's fascination with him is unequivocally clear.

Ed Wood also gave Tim Burton another opportunity to work on his own *biographical project* — by focusing on the relationship between Bela Lugosi and Wood, for example, which virtually mirrors Burton's own relationship with Vincent Price. Ed Wood shot the last scenes of *Plan 9 from Outer Space* with Bela Lugosi shortly before the old man died. Burton captured a conversation with Vincent Price — his last cinematic testament — on celluloid and it lies, as yet unreleased, in Burton's archives. Burton's identification with the life and work of Ed Wood is therefore hardly surprising: 'One of the things I liked about Ed, and I could relate to, was being passionate about what you do to the point of it becoming like a weird drug... But you thinking you're doing the greatest thing in the world maybe doesn't have anything to do with how the rest of the population perceives it' (*Burton on Burton*, Mark Salisbury).

The scene in which Bela Lugosi stands in front of his house in his black cape, somewhat unsteadily walks across to the flowerbed and smells a rose is one of the most touching sequences in Burton's film. It has a nostalgic, sentimental tone which isn't really found elsewhere in *Ed Wood* — we are witnessing the last act of a representative of a dying age, capturing its erstwhile greatness one last time. Bela's days are numbered, like those of the flower he places in his lapel; his pride is battered, but not broken. The scene makes us forget Lugosi's less than glorious demise, and is an expression of Burton's deep respect for the actor.

In their efforts to bring that era back to life, Burton and his producer and longstanding colleague Denise Di Novi had to take a few liberties, and not just in dealing with the biographical facts. Actors often say that comedy is more difficult to perform than tragedy, but what about something that was unintentionally funny, like Wood's films? Burton must have found it correspondingly difficult to reconstruct Ed Wood's dilettante style. It's one thing not to be able to do something any better, but quite another to do it deliberately badly.

...and the same scenes in the original *Plan 9*

The originals: Criswell, Vampira, Tor Johnson, Bunny Breckinridge

Burton had eighteen million dollars at his disposal to achieve it — many times more than the production expenses of all Ed Wood's films put together. Some of the best technicians in Hollywood, many of whom Burton had worked with before, were involved in *Ed Wood*, including Stefan Czapsky, the German-born cameraman who had already run photography on *Edward Scissorhands* and *Batman Returns,* and the award-winning make-up artists Rick Baker and Ve Neill (*Beetle Juice*), reliable comrades in arms whose advice Tim Burton was always willing to listen to. The decision to shoot the film in black and white, for example, was a result of make-up tests with Martin Landau, who won an Oscar for his interpretation of the Bela Lugosi role, as Burton explained: 'Rick [Baker] said: "What colour are Bela's eyes?" and we realised that none of us had seen Lugosi in colour' (*Film Comment*, 11-12/1994). It was quickly decided that Johnny Depp should play the role of Ed Wood, but the rest of the casting proved to be a long drawn-out process. The aim was to find actors who resembled the originals as closely as possible, but it was very difficult to find a modern-day equivalent for either Tor Johnson or Vampira. In the end, Lisa Marie, Burton's real life partner, was just right for the part of the mysterious Vampira, and they hit the nail on the head again with George 'The Animal' Steele, alias Jim Myers, a gigantic wrestler of the same proportions as the original colossus who imitates Johnson's brutish acting style excellently. Also worthy of mention is Bill Murray's precise portrayal of Bunny

Breckinridge, the transsexual — only through his exquisite manner can a contrast be drawn with Wood's clumsy cross-dressing.

Burton's film is an attempt to create a simulacrum, a faithful copy of Wood's world. Apart from the spirit and the personal touch, which Tim Burton was responsible for, they had to make replicas of the sparse, shaky sets of three of the old master's films. A costly enterprise, even though Ed Wood had made do with props which happened to be to hand, cheap junk borrowed from friends or acquired by other means (such as the giant octopus, which, according to rumour, was *borrowed* from the store of Republic Studios). For *Ed Wood*, everything had to be tailor-made, constructed anew or somehow conjured up from the treasure chests of Hollywood.

There is a touch of irony inherent in going to such enormous lengths to replicate the work of a rank amateur who was never so much loved or loathed but ignored by Hollywood. And there is a somewhat tragic pathos about the reception of this 'very good film about a very bad film-maker', as the *New York Times* put it, especially if one takes into account the irony that the story about the man who never achieved financial or critical success himself brought work, money and fame to others years on. It made Michael Medved, the man behind the Golden Turkey Award, into a television film critic, who, funnily enough, has since taken up the defence of traditional family values. On the basis of Rudolph Grey's book, two documentary

The copies: Jeffrey Jones, Lisa Marie, George Steele, Bill Murray

films were made about Ed Wood, *Ed Wood — Look Back in Angora* (1994, dir. Ted Newson) and *The Haunted World of Edward D. Wood Jr* (1996, dir. Brett Thompson) — in which the old veterans line up and give an account of themselves. A CD of the complete soundtrack of *Plan 9 from Outer Space* has been released and a video documentary — *Flying Saucers over Hollywood: The Plan 9 Companion* (1992, dir. Mark Patrick Carducci) — has been put together. There is also the comedy *Plan 10 from Outer Space* (1994, dir. Trent Harris), a spoof fifties science fiction film about Mormon cosmology shot in Salt Lake City, Utah.

But what is the result of this recent exploitation of exploitation? And what does it mean to make a good film about a lousy director whose films were so bad they're almost good, as the saying goes? In Tim Burton's case, what he has produced is an ode to a loser's unswerving need for cinematic self-expression, an ode which also satisfies the spectators' need for anti-heroes and the schlock aesthetic. Burton narrowly avoids the trap of recreating the past through rose-coloured spectacles, depicting real characters as naïve and innocent, by judicious use of irony. Curiously, however, *Ed Wood* seems formally much less like a B-movie than some scenes from *Batman,* for example, because nothing was left to chance. Tim Burton recreated the world of Ed Wood with a steady hand and perfect control — his consummate sense of style and attention to detail won him the highest honours in the cinematic world. What does, in the end, turn *Ed Wood* into a B-movie is the lack of respect for Ed himself, for the man he actually was. Burton's approach is in fact exploitative because of the (well-intentioned) avoidance of the ultimate tragedy and pathos of Wood's life. In the end, Burton turns his subject into kitsch.

Mars Attacks! — Attack on the Laughter Muscles

A film genre which was particularly popular in the seventies, and which has enjoyed a recent revival of fortune, is the disaster movie. Films like tornado drama *Twister* (1996, dir. Jan De Bont) and the blockbuster epic *Titanic* (1997, dir. James Cameron) are only the tip of the cinema-of-disaster iceberg, allowing Hollywood another opportunity to show off its skills at producing crowd-pleasing special effects, lavish sets, costumes and make-up. Mayhem reigns in disaster movies, and effects specialists jump at the chance to stage such bravura scenes. The wild, untameable elements, dreadful disasters on land, afloat and in the air, fires, earthquakes, bomb blasts — this is the stuff of catastrophic disaster movie scenarios, reproduced in as much lurid detail as possible. It is one of the most fundamentally American of film genres and there's always a lot at stake — not least the fate of the entire human race!

When Tim Burton was developing *Mars Attacks!*, he had in mind a classic disaster movie in the mode of Irwin Allen, the director/producer of *Voyage to the Bottom of the Sea* (1961) and *The Poseidon Adventure* (1972, dir. Ronald Neame). Armies of aliens, extras and explosions were just his style. 'It was during the Gulf War when the media seemed to have reached a new level. Wars with titles and musical themes — I found that a bit disturbing' (*Premiere*, 1/1997). The time seemed right for a satire of America's catastrophe culture, a

satire with a subversive message which would pour scorn on public institutions, including the President, the military and the media industry, as well as on the disaster genre itself.

The aliens are coming: *Independence Day* (Jeff Goldblum), *Starship Troopers* (Denise Richards, Patrick Muldoon), *Contact* (Jodie Foster)

Around the same time as *Mars Attacks!*, a glut of expensively produced sci-fi disasters stormed cinemas in the mid-nineties. They all dealt with the same subject — alien invasion — and they each, in their own way, reworked the American dream of the constant search for new frontiers. In this country, where the West ends on Sunset Boulevard and the natural boundary that is the Pacific Ocean, there's only one direction left — upwards! The enthusiasm for all things extraterrestrial took on ludicrous forms, attracting the reverence and spiritual significance of a religion. Talk-shows were full of enlightened witnesses, who claimed to have sighted UFOs and even been abducted by their occupants. Crop circles were discovered in corn fields, and nobody could explain how they came about. Photographs of aliens were circulated on the Internet — beings with friendly eyes, delicate fingers and a suspiciously close resemblance to Steven Spielberg's ET. In an era of increasing demystification and secularisation, new miracles had to be found, clarifying the connection between *science* and *fiction* in the run-up to the new millennium.

Thus, occupation film *Independence Day* (1996), from German director Roland Emmerich, came along at exactly the right time, although the special effects received more attention than the simple, patriotic story. Paul Verhoeven's *Starship Troopers* (1997), on the other hand, was a rather questionable totalitarian fantasy involving earthlings attacking hostile extraterrestrial beings. The anti-democratic slant of Robert A. Heinlein's original novel was carried through to the film, and even the almost Burton-esque inserts in the style of weekly news reports didn't manage to lift the darker subtext. *Contact* (1997, dir. Robert Zemeckis) and *Sphere* (1998, dir. Barry Levinson), two relatively intelligent films, also explore the possibilities involved in encounters of the third kind, with a touch of scepticism in the answers they offer. While *Contact* shows a trip into a scientist's consciousness (and the realm of astrophysics, emphatically defended in the film, acquires the status of *l'art pour l'art*), *Sphere* declares everything extraterrestrial to be part of the unconscious, projections of the protagonists themselves.

Such distance and scepticism with regard to the inexplicable was unthinkable in classic science fiction. Rather more common was a heavy-handed demonstration of the technological and intellectual superiority of human beings — the military enjoyed flexing its muscles and displaying advanced weapons systems — the rationale and detailed scientific explanations behind the action, often presented in the style of an educational film, were not always of great interest to the audience. American science fiction of the fifties, *Invaders from Mars* (1953, dir. William Cameron Menzies), for example, or *This Island Earth* (1955, dir. Joseph M. Newman), displays great innocence in the face of a modern, progressive world — an inno-

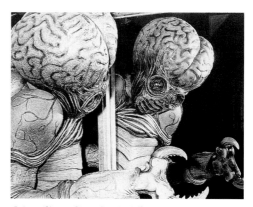

Sphere (Sharon Stone, Dustin Hoffman), *Invaders from Mars*, *This Island Earth*

cence today's films have lost. In *Mars Attacks!*, Tim Burton refers explicitly to the naïve science fiction movies he watched in his youth. His film departs from the contemporary model and gently frees itself from the restrictions of the genre and the attendant ideological baggage. Instead, *Mars Attacks!* makes fun of a lot of things which are sacred to other people. If it's true that science fiction is always about the repressed, about our own desires and fears, and what film critic Georg Seesslen calls, 'the inner aggression we're not sure how to deal with properly' (*epd Film*, 1/1997), this view acquires a new meaning in *Mars Attacks!*.

Every genre reaches its zenith at a particular point in time and within a particular social context; further progress inevitably suffers a consequent loss of meaning. Over a period of time, the science fiction film replaced the Western, when the latter no longer encountered gold in the promised land but rather the cynicism of capitalism, and the genre lost its way in the land of the free. In its stead, the science fiction film tried its luck in remote worlds where it ultimately found nothing but the reflection of its own motives, frequently amounting to a simple desire to flee. Science fiction movies represented a vision — the dream of universal harmony, intimated even in the genre's many negative utopias. (The fear of unleashed technologies, atom bombs, epidemics and dictatorships is in the end also an expression of the desire for a safe world free of such things — whether it actually exists 'out there' somewhere, or has to be devised by human beings first.) This dream apparently died out, but the contemporary science fiction film articulates the same urge in very different ways: on the one hand, by acting as if nothing had happened (*Independence Day, Starship Troopers*), and, on the other, by revealing a late twentieth century scepticism about its own motivation (*Contact, Sphere*). Tim Burton stands for a third option, demolishing both versions with barely concealed relish.

Nuke 'em now!

Mars Attacks! sets out its stall right away. The pre-credits sequence sees a farmer and his Chinese neighbour in Lockjaw, Kentucky startled by a herd of burning cows galloping down the highway. Mad cow disease? Shortly after, a UFO takes off from behind the house and sets out for Mars via the movie credits. The scene is derived from the fifty-five part series of collector's cards issued by the Topps Chewing Gum Company in 1962 and rereleased in 1994. They were hugely popular when they first came out — despite being withdrawn from sale after six months because their depictions of scenarios such as 'Destroying a Dog' or 'Burning Flesh' were felt to be too violent. Nonetheless, they inspired British scriptwriter Jonathan Gems to explore the colourful world of catastrophe which became, under Tim Burton's direction, a milestone in live-action cartoonery. The watchword, or aesthetic premise, as it were, was *low-concept* — everything was to look as cheap as possible, as cheesy as the old B-movies Tim Burton remembered with such affection.

An armada of UFOs moves in from Mars — hundreds of funny, silver saucers on a geometric path to Earth, which they proceed to surround. The hotline to Washington is already buzzing and the President of the United States, James Dale (Jack Nicholson), sees his most glorious hour approaching. His liberal advisers, press spokesman Jerry Ross (Martin Short) and scientist Professor Donald Kessler (Pierce Brosnan), persuade him that it would be wrong to assume that the Martians' intentions are hostile, and the beleaguered President follows their advice. Instead of

Violent: Topps collector's cards

A crowd of famous actors: (left) Glenn Close, Annette Bening, Pierce Brosnan, Jim Brown; (right) Danny DeVito, Lukas Haas, Michael J. Fox, Pam Grier

the shoot-to-kill policy favoured by governments in classic science fiction stories (as recommended by choleric General Decker [Rod Steiger], usually at the top of his voice), they decide to fight a media battle for programme ratings and votes. The Martians could just turn out to be the answer to the prayers of the President and his wife (Glenn Close), evidently modelled on former First Lady Nancy Reagan.

As is only proper in a good disaster movie, several subplots unfold in different places at the same time. The news that the Earth has been surrounded has already done the rounds of the media. In the gambling city of Las Vegas, a property shark, appropriately called Art Land (also Jack Nicholson), is already rubbing his hands in anticipation of the business he can do on the back of the extraterrestrial tourists. His wife

(Left) Tom Jones, Sarah Jessica Parker, Martin Short, Sylvia Sydney; (right) Rod Steiger, Barbet Schroeder, Jack Nicholson in dual roles

Barbara (Annette Bening), an alcoholic going through an esoteric phase, wants to prepare herself spiritually for the visitors and is meditating furiously in the lotus position. A former professional boxer working as security in a casino is trying to get to his wife in Washington DC (the couple are played by blaxploitation icons Jim Brown and Pam Grier). Meanwhile, the broadcasting networks are taking up their positions in the Nevada Desert, awaiting the arrival of the Martians. 'Boulevard' presenter Nathalie Lake (Sarah Jessica Parker) and her boyfriend, 'GNN' reporter Jason Stone (Michael J. Fox), arrive, privately connected though professionally in competition — the tabloids against the serious press, always a safe bet for Burton. To Jason's great annoyance, Nathalie manages to entice Presidential adviser Professor Kessler into her studio, where he declares: 'This is the most important thing to happen since, perhaps, Jesus walked in Galilee.' The hysteria is whipped up to such a degree that even in Perkinsville, Kansas, in the Midwest where, traditionally, nothing happens, a family prepares to send their eldest son into battle for the defence of civilisation. Their youngest son Richie (Lukas Haas) is not allowed to play the hero, however, as he has to look after his aged grandmother (Sylvia Sidney). It's all the more ironic that the solution to the crisis actually comes from this improbable, marginalised pair, in the form of dreadful, deafening Hillbilly yodel 'Indian Love Call' by Slim Whitman, which even Martians can't stand.

Genre attacks

Film critics have often compared *Mars Attacks!* with *Independence Day* because of their very similar scenarios, 'but Roland Emmerich and Tim Burton's different approaches to the story shows that there are worlds between them' (*epd Film*, 3/1197). There is an ocean, a continent and a few mountain ranges separating them, at least. Five months after Emmerich's hugely successful disaster film, *Mars Attacks!* must have seemed like a parody, although there was no direct relation between the two movies. Unlike Emmerich, the newcomer to America, Tim Burton, the American renegade, dispenses with the patriotic conventions usually so central to the disaster genre. Quite the contrary, in fact — Burton maintains his dissident spirit, featuring a Mexican Mariachi band playing a particularly oblique version of American national anthem 'The Star Spangled Banner' at the end of the movie, commenting on the precarious balance of multi-racial America, one which doesn't just provoke discord with people from distant galaxies. Where Emmerich bravely holds on to an American dream, as only fairly well-off immigrants can still hope to, Burton, who was no doubt amused by Emmerich's naïve populism, preferred to throw a spanner in the works with *Mars Attacks!*, an uncompromising deconstruction and critique of Hollywood cinema costing seventy million dollars.

One ought to credit Burton's actors, a crew full of famous names to whom dreadful things happen one after another — they all pass away amazingly quickly, dying rather ignominious deaths, which Burton once described as 'cathartic' (*Premiere*, 1/1997), brought low by enormous chandeliers or torpedoed by Martians. Only the less well-known stars playing smaller roles are allowed to survive — a rather unusual way of proceeding in Hollywood. Burton was also able to

Exeunt the stars: Glenn Close's premature passing

play with his actor's established images, effectively casting stars such as Tom Jones and Rod Steiger as caricatures of their own public personas. It's not often that actors enjoy themselves so much in a film — especially Glenn Close and Jack Nicholson as the Presidential couple.

Despite the use of advanced computer technology, the production design relies on Burton's customary cheap chic. Initially, the animated scenes were to be produced in stop-motion, and a team of British animators had already been assembled when Industrial Light and Magic, George Lucas' famous computer effects factory, took over for financial reasons. The large-scale and expensive film, however, shows no ill effects from the switch to computer animation, as Burton played up the virtual artificiality with a kind of comicbook realism. The green (naturally) Martians look like toy soldiers, and their weapons resemble top-of-the-range water pistols. Their leader wears a glamorous red cape, modelled on the wrap Gloria Swanson wore in her famous role as Norma Desmond, the ageing silent film diva in *Sunset Boulevard* (1950, dir. Billy Wilder). That film was about the leap into the era of sound cinema, which some stars were unable to make, and which heralded the death knell of the silent film.

Tim Burton was able to move forward and leave the conventions of the science fiction film lying in his wake. *Mars Attacks!* caricatures not only the patriotic, military tradition of the alien invasion film, but also its 'liberal' alternative, which approaches the aliens with pacifist and spiritually motivated goodwill. A deliberately symbolic image shows a New Age disciple launching a dove into the air as a sign of friendship on the day the Martians land. The dove of peace is also a reference to Steven Spielberg's *Close Encounters of the Third Kind* (1977), which uses doves in an experiment involving some kind of mysterious radiation.

The Martian leader deciphers a message

Unfamiliar with Earthly symbolism, the Martians in Burton's film interpret the greeting as a pre-emptive strike from the military and open fire. Did Professor Kessler not claim that a highly developed civilisation couldn't, by definition, be barbaric? The subsequent inferno is adequate punishment for his misjudgement. Burton slaughters all those who intended to profit from the encounter — television reporters chasing high ratings; young soldiers fantasising about Vietnam; a General thirsting for the limelight who actually shrinks to the size of his true significance before being trampled by the Martians; and finally a President whom the Martians zap with one of their lethal laser beams even as he moves them to tears, mouthing appeasing words and making imploring gestures. The Disney-esque final scene, featuring Tom Jones belting out his evergreen 'It's Not Unusual' with an eagle on his arm in front of a kitsch mountain background, while the world

Misinterpretation: the Martians' response to the pacifist welcome (and Burton's response to *Wild at Heart*)

lies in ruins all around him, is particularly ironic. The conclusion of *Mars Attacks!* provides no resolution to the confusion of the whole.

This puzzle was not particularly well received by either the critics or the public. The former reproached Burton fairly unanimously for his usual failings — particularly his tendency to focus in on individual scenes rather than the bigger picture, although some put that

down to the influence of his model, Topps' series of collector's cards. Audiences stayed away from the cinemas over Christmas 1996, though video and DVD sales made up for this, as *Mars Attacks!* has become a key film due to its references and special effects. Although word went round that Tim Burton might be following in the unfortunate footsteps of his hero, Ed Wood, that's actually the point of this exceedingly enjoyable film: '*Mars Attacks!* is intended as a kind of anti-entertainment, a subversion of the production values of the major studios, of the fame of stars and of the polished illusions of movies like *Independence Day*. In a certain sense this film, together with *Ed Wood*, is Tim Burton's declaration of independence from the expectations created by the success of the *Batman* film' (*New Yorker*, 16/12/96).

Danny Elfman's Film Music

by Dirk Schaefer

A Tim Burton film almost always has music by Danny Elfman — from *Pee-wee's Big Adventure* to *Sleepy Hollow*, all of Burton's movies (with the exception of *Ed Wood*) over fourteen years have borne the musical signature of former rock musician Danny Elfman. Such creative partnerships are common throughout film history — one has only to think of the longstanding collaboration between Alfred Hitchcock and Bernard Herrmann, or Federico Fellini and Nino Rota; and more recently, creative teams like David Lynch and Angelo Badalamenti, David Cronenberg and Howard Shore, and, of course, Peter Greenaway and Michael Nyman. When it comes to the tricky question of setting his or her films to music, the *auteur* seems to look to a kindred soul rather than a solid, but ultimately interchangeable, craftsman. While directors such as Hitchcock, Lynch or Burton are perceived as artists who think particularly visually, they also frequently have their own characteristic sound signature, as Elizabeth Weis shows in her book dealing exclusively with Alfred Hitchcock's use of music and his 'Expressionist' way with sound effects, as well as his tendency to integrate pieces of music into the plot even as the script is being drafted (habits which are shared, as we shall see, by Tim Burton). If a director uses a previously more or less well-known piece of music, he or she must take the various connotations of that music into consideration (the way Hitchcock plays with the Léhar waltz 'The Merry Widow' in *Shadow of a Doubt* [1943], for example). Music composed especially for a film, on the other

Danny Elfman

hand, brings its own risks as well as the obvious advantages, since 'the composition of the music is the aspect of film-making over which directors have the least control' (*The Silent Scream: Alfred Hitchcock's Soundtrack*, Elizabeth Weis). A director like Burton, who doesn't simply want to leave the music for his films to its own devices, will prefer to entrust its composition to someone who sees things as he does. Finding the right colleagues could be a matter of sheer luck, but Burton has a system...

Before we turn specifically to the music of Danny Elfman, let's briefly consider what Tim Burton's films sound like *without* him.

Illusion and irony

A boy in his bedroom, lost in thought, the door occasionally opened by his mother, vainly trying to persuade him to come out — this is the tableau at the heart of *Vincent*. This theme reappears again and again in the more personal works of the director, if a little less starkly. It's no doubt a reference to certain childhood memories Burton associated with Edgar Allan Poe, Vincent Price and the idea of being buried alive, literally or metaphorically.

In a revealing reversal of this scenario, it's Burton's (anti-) heroes who actually lock themselves in. Burton's films, from *Vincent* to *Ed Wood*, are always art about art, and they constantly (and perhaps out of necessity) take up the defence of the imagination in the conflict between the inside and outside, between fantasy and reality. This is where the soundtrack comes in. In the case of *Vincent*, the gloomy, droning organ music (composed by Ken Hilton) helps the grotesque visions imagined by the child (and Burton) acquire a certain intensity, and at the same time conjures up the atmosphere of a horror film starring Vincent Price — only to be strangled at a stroke by the sound of the door when banal reality in the shape of the mother breaks in: 'Come out, it's a beautiful day.' When she closes the door, the ghost (and the music) start up again, and so on. This abrupt switch from one mood to another is a stylistic device typical of cartoon music, which shadows every turn of events — it achieves a comic effect, but often at the expense of unity. In an animated film such as *Vincent*, it's noticeable how the music and sound effects are used as counterparts. Music represents the world of Vincent's mind, and what is perhaps a threatening excess of imagination. The cartoon-like, exaggerated sound of the door, on the other hand, chases away the spirits conjured up by the film and the music itself. What Burton builds up with one hand, the music, he knocks down again with the other, the sound effects. This technique of shattering illusions and atmospheres is known as Romantic irony; the music allows us to enjoy an expansive emotional state, but at the same time the counterpoint of the banal is always there, waiting to surface. Again and again,

The spook in *Vincent*

Burton introduces incarnations of the mundane into his films in the shape of rather dull characters (apart from Alfred, Bruce Wayne's butler in the *Batman* films, these characters are usually women) with a normal, healthy attitude, somewhat boring, who try to pull the hero out of his splendid isolation. Lacking imagination, their appearance frequently destroys the magic just conjured up by the music.

Frankenweenie (music by Michael Convertino and David Newman) once again takes up this theme of the contrast between expansive emotions one can indulge in with the aid of music, and the more pragmatically inclined mother figure. In one scene, the boy is standing sadly at the window after his dog has been buried, when the rain sets in, pattering against the window and

Funereal music in *Frankenweenie*

creating a classic, melodramatically mournful mood; on the soundtrack we hear appropriately funereal music from the string section. This carefully constructed shot, swelling with emotion and sad music, is then countered by an illusion-shattering view from outside — what appeared to be rain is in fact water from his mother's garden hose, revealed as the camera slowly pulls back from the window, the tragic music fading away until all one can hear is the water on the glass — a cold shower for the overheated feelings of the hero, to whom his mother seems to be saying, indirectly, 'Life goes on'. In *Vincent*, one can assume that the weepie music would have been turned off more brutally. Burton is working much more subtly with the possibilities afforded by film music here, though one should also say that he now had much more money at his disposal, so the two composers were in a position to use orchestral music in Hollywood's late Romantic style, without worrying about the expense.

Pee-wee's Big Adventure is a variation on this basic motif. Burton's first feature film, it also marks the beginning of his collaboration with Danny Elfman, with a dream sequence in which Pee-wee, in his grey suit as ever, wins the Tour de France. The ringing of the alarm clock insinuates its way like an unwanted guest into the 'dreamy' music accompanying the victory celebrations and, rather than the dream coming to an abrupt end, it's affected more and more by the intrusion of everyday life — the imaginary people celebrating Pee-wee's victory flee *within* the dream and

leave him alone, then the dream and the music stop while the alarm carries on ringing as our hero wakes up in his bed.

And the mother figure? The part that the mothers play in the lives of Vincent and Victor is filled by Dottie, Pee-wee's obtrusive friend. In terms of sound, this is discreetly indicated by the fact that Dottie's attempts to flirt with Pee-wee are never set to music. The more positive side of Dottie's ambivalent role becomes clear when Pee-wee tries to organise a search for his stolen bicycle with his assembled friends, behaving like a mad scientist getting over-excited about his crazy ideas. The score underlines this process with ghostly music of the spheres; when Pee-wee, his friends already leaving him, shaking their heads, suddenly shuts down, saying over and

Mad scientist: Pee-wee calls for a search for his bicycle

Plea for sanity: Dolores Fuller and Ed Wood

over like a broken record, 'It's like you're unravelling a big sweater and someone keeps knitting... and knitting... and knitting...', the music also sticks, repeating the same phrase again and again. Dottie proves to be his last faithful follower and pulls him out of his trance — at which point the music suddenly stops.

The tension between inside and outside, a fundamental feature of Burton's films, is also audible on the soundtrack of *Ed Wood*, as a conflict between self-destructive men who refuse to grow up and mothering female characters lacking either imagination or music. The horror film director, himself another kind of mad scientist, is stopped in his tracks by his girl-friend in front of the assembled film crew — respectable Dolores loses her rag when Ed celebrates his new film by dancing in drag to ecstatic mambo music. She screams the truth into the silence at the end of the song: 'Nobody will watch this film. It's disgusting!'. Wood, of course, doesn't allow this alarm call from healthy normality to impinge any further on him. Just as Vincent Malloy insists that he's Vincent Price, Ed Wood thinks he's the Orson Welles of trash. The fact that, after Burton's film, we are inclined to think he may have been right is due in no small part to Howard Shore's music, which lifts the convincingly depicted shabbiness into the realm of tragic failure. When Bela Lugosi (Martin Landau) intones absurd monologues in his thick accent, the heavily sentimental music accompanying the scene lends the music hall tricks a certain real magic — invoking the wonder of pure film-making, without the involvement of either money, sense or talent.

Californian pallor

In the words of Tim Burton, a director and his composer should be 'in sync', just like the pictures and the sound; matched up beforehand, not afterwards. Agreeing on a piece of music and what it expresses is really a matter of luck and chance, and all the more so if you are not, as per Burton's frequently expressed self-description, a man of words. But Burton's luck in choosing long-term collaborators appears to be the result of a system of choosing personalities he connects with. Henry Selick, director of *The Nightmare Before Christmas*, makes this clear when he says: 'I got the job because Tim and I come from the same planet — if not the same neighbourhood' (*Tim Burton's The Nightmare Before Christmas — The Film, the Art, the Vision*, Frank Thompson). It's also worth noting the reason Burton put forward for casting Michelle Pfeiffer as the Catwoman, namely her southern Californian background: 'She's from Orange County, a kind of similar era and similar environment to mine, and maybe I connected with her on that level' (*Burton on Burton*, Mark Salisbury).

If a common background was still significant when working with top people such as Selick and Pfeiffer, then being on the same wavelength really was important in finding the composer for *Pee-wee's Big Adventure*. When Burton and Paul Reubens decided on Danny Elfman, they were choosing a rock musician who was completely unknown in the film industry, but whose band Oingo Boingo had a cult following — including Tim Burton. Four years older than Burton, and brought up in a middle class household in Baldwin Hills, Los Angeles, Danny Elfman is, according to Joshua A. Fruhlinger, 'just like the rest of us who grew up in the suburban sprawl called southern

Oingo Boingo record covers

Buried alive: Pee-wee's chock-a-block room

California' (*Pluggage*). This 'us' doesn't refer to the classic image of sun-tanned teenagers with surfboards (what Elfman calls 'repulsive teenagers... the kind of people I've spent my life hiding from' [*Pluggage*]), of course, but their quieter counterparts, the pale nerds who take refuge from the endless summer in bedrooms stuffed with records, film posters and technical gadgets — buried alive in LA. 'I always had this dislike of sun,' says Elfman, and '*MTV Beach House* is my idea of hell.' In the land of eternal summer, the stay-at-home is virtually a rebel, pale skin almost a statement. It's this Californian pallor which connects Danny Elfman with Tim Burton, and also with Pee-wee Herman and Edward Scissorhands, and has made possible a level of co-operation characterised by unconditional trust.

Work with Burton functions on an 'intuitive' level, according to Elfman in conversation with Kevin Allmann: 'Rather than telling me exactly what he wants orchestrally, Tim will show me a scene and describe the feeling he wants to get across. Then I'll go into the studio and try to find that feeling in music' (*Details*, 12/1993).

In this search for suitable musical expression, Elfman makes use of childhood memories of Hollywood cinema as it used to be; coming from the same cultural background as Burton, it was his first love even before music came along. Unlike the great film composers he admires — Max Steiner, Nino Rota and, of course, Bernard Herrmann — Elfman didn't come to film through classical music but rather as a film fan and a connoisseur of soundtracks. 'I'm extremely ignorant about classical music, unlike film music', he once admitted to the industry magazine *Soundtrack!* — or, to make it even clearer: 'I grew up on movies, not "music".'

One could even say of Danny Elfman the film composer (as opposed to Elfman the director — he signed a two-picture writing/directing deal with Disney in

1999, the first film composer to make the jump to Hollywood director) that he grew up in public. Burton, the novice director, was surrounded with experienced professionals by concerned film producers on *Pee-wee's Big Adventure*, and, along with Elfman, has since managed to maintain a close-knit team of talented individuals within the system. Burton frankly admits to having learnt the craft of film-making in the director's chair: 'As you go along you learn about lenses. It's taken me a while but I gather information each time. You just try to keep learning on a basic technical level' *(Burton on Burton*, Mark Salisbury); Elfman gets the desired cinematic, orchestral sound (the actual instrumentation) from long-standing colleague and expert Steve Bartek. However satisfying it is to hear the music which has been sweated over on the piano or keyboard finally being played by a big orchestra, the matching up of direction and music takes place within Elfman's own four walls. After the preparatory spotting sessions during which the director jots down a few thoughts (such as how much music is required at particular points in the film, what it should convey, which existing songs are heard by the characters in certain scenes), it's over to the composer. As always, Burton places great emphasis on the unspoken understanding between them: '[Elfman] got a tape of the film [*Pee-wee's Big Adventure*] and I would go over to his house and he'd play little things on his keyboard so I could see it right there. We were definitely on the same wavelength. It was good because what he couldn't verbalise, or what I couldn't verbalise, didn't matter because it was *there*, and he got it' *(Burton on Burton*, Mark Salisbury).

Clearly, the hierarchy within the film industry allows certain auteurs to establish a recognisable style which can be executed well by creative colleagues — the main thing is that all involved have an idea of how a Tim Burton film should look and how a Danny Elfman score should sound.

Influences: Max Steiner, Nino Rota, Bernard Herrmann

And how does the whole thing sound, then? In short, it sounds like film music. With an approach similar to Burton's, Elfman puts his music together out of clichés and echoes of (and, more rarely, phrases taken directly from) the work of predecessors he admires. Elfman's music is not entirely self-contained, and it constantly evokes memories, ringing a bell, as it were, in the listener. For instance, Nino Rota's style may have been the model for the circus-like music at the beginning of *Pee-wee's Big Adventure*; Pee-wee reacts to the theft of his beloved bicycle with despair, and Elfman matches it with shrilly shrieking music for strings — a somewhat inappropriate homage to Bernard Herrmann's shower-murder music for Hitchcock's *Psycho*; the siren sounds signalling just how bewildered Pee-wee has become in the meantime remind us of science fiction B-movies like *It Came from Outer Space* (1953, dir. Jack Arnold); and, finally, the film version of his own experiences Pee-wee watches on the big screen at the end is accompanied by the flashy, sexy, blue notes of wind instruments sounding like a James Bond theme by John Barry. Full of enthusiasm, Burton suggests that the most important element of Elfman's work is that the music effectively becomes a character of its own (*Burton on Burton*, Mark Salisbury). In fact, it seems to act more like a multiple personality, frequently bordering on slapstick, the music playfully jumping from one pose to another, just like Pee-wee himself. The method in this madness is also known as cartoon music.

When Warner Bros launched their own cartoons as an alternative to the good clean fun of their competitors, Disney, the music they used was anything but 'childish', and was full of sophisticated references. Typical cartoon music, especially as developed by Carl Stalling in the thirties and forties, is characterised by funny noises and musical references, from contemporary hits to well-worn standards. Composers writing for cartoons can only laugh at the notion that film music should subtly, discreetly lend support to the pictures on screen. 'What's the good of it if you can't hear it?' asked Elfman's favourite composer, Max Steiner, who indirectly introduced the techniques of cartoon music into 'real film' via the soundtrack of fantasy spectacle *King Kong* (1933, dir. Merian C. Cooper, Ernest B. Schoedsack). Steiner stuck to his habit of following the actors' movements with the music, which was soon criticised by Hollywood producers like David O. Selznick as 'Mickey Mousing'. Unfortunately, tricks which heightened the illusion of movement in animation had the opposite effect on a film with real actors. There might have been some sense to aping movements musically when King Kong falls off the top of the Empire State Building, but not when Bette Davis trips down a few steps.

However, many of Tim Burton's films started out in life as cartoon-like drawings — not just *Edward Scissorhands*, which was originally a sketch by the director, but above all the two *Batman* films. Elfman's signature, his preference — inherited from Steiner — for following the action with music, his neglect of the bigger picture in favour of the miniature, the cartoony approach which became more and more refined after *Pee-wee*, is completely at odds with the reality-enhancing scoring expected from a modern action film, however close it may be to a live-action cartoon. *Batman* — a film which neither Burton nor Elfman were particularly happy with — is a fine example of the problems inherent in walking a tightrope between illusion and irony on the soundtrack of a Hollywood blockbuster.

The soundtrack albums for *Edward Scissorhands*, *Batman* and *Batman Returns*

Batman: action cracker or comicbook?

'**W**hat I find fault with most these days is our inability to compose soundtracks for action films... Each time I tried it I was terribly disappointed in the end,' said Elfman in 1993, disillusioned

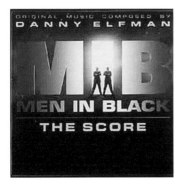

Film music by Danny Elfman: *Darkman,*
Good Will Hunting, Men in Black

following his rapid rise as composer for a series of fantasy action films (*Batman, Dick Tracy* [1990, dir. Warren Beatty], *Darkman* [1990, dir. Sam Raimi], *Batman Returns*). Despite his disappointment, Elfman has remained faithful to the genre up to now. Although he's made successful excursions into drama (*Dolores Claiborne* [1995, dir. Taylor Hackford], for example, or *Good Will Hunting* [1997, dir. Gus van Sant], for which he was nominated for an Academy Award), Elfman is still primarily identified with the scores of films like *Mars Attacks!* and *Men in Black* (1997, dir. Barry Sonnenfeld), which earned him a further Oscar nomination. In the light of the clear and continued success which followed Elfman's work on *Batman*, one wonders whether the 'failure' has not been programmed into the work from the start — whether it doesn't lie in his desire to be old-fashioned and modern at the same time, as he once described his vision. It's the music particularly which places *Batman* in the tradition of the big adventure movie. After being frequently pronounced dead in the sixties and seventies, classic Hollywood film music in the late Romantic style has been enjoying an almost uninterrupted revival since *Star Wars* (1977, dir. George Lucas) and *Raiders of the Lost Ark* (1981, dir. Steven Spielberg).

Elfman expresses his admiration of the composer John Williams, whose work on *Star Wars* and *Raiders of the Lost Ark*, he says, 'defined the "super-hero" music of our generation, and he took the lead from Erich Wolfgang Korngold, who composed great heroic scores like *The Adventures of Robin Hood* [1938, dir. Michael Curtiz, William Keighley]' (*Soundtrack!*, 9/1992). Funnily enough, writer Royal S. Brown describes an Elfman score as 'Erich Korngold via John Williams' (*Overtones and Undertones*, Royal S. Brown). Elfman provided the title sequence for *Batman* (an animated tracking shot around dark vaults which turn out to be the inside of the Batman logo) with a soundtrack quite in the spirit of the opera composer Korngold, who liked to treat the opening scenes as an overture. Beginning with the Warner logo and ending with the Batman logo, the introductory sequence, the connection between the advertising campaign and the product, and also between the cinema advertisements and the main film, evokes the splendour of the golden age of cinema — this is to be nothing less than a re-birth, including the journey through the birth canal. In an effort to distinguish itself from an evening at home in front of the television — and television sets get a bad deal in *Batman*! — the cinema celebrates itself here as a community experience, audible in the swelling sound of the seventy-five piece orchestra. Like Korngold or Steiner, Elfman's music follows the movement on screen, even during the introduction: the music begins (with the *Batman* theme) when the very first image, the Warner Bros logo, appears, with a fanfare over the title. The camera starts to move, and so does the music, shifting from an ominous droning, already an indication of the dark side of the hero, to a march, and then reaching a climax on the appearance of the *Batman* logo. This crescendo is so well-timed that it carries us through the fading of the logo into the black background and then leads into the first, establishing shot of the metropolis with the subtitle 'Gotham City' — curtain up!

It's no coincidence that Elfman's music makes its first and most effective appearance before and outside of the actual plot, for the sound of Gotham City proves to be a Babylonian cacophony of scraps of music, noises and speech. Over the course of the film, songs from Prince's soundtrack album, as well as easy listening music from the Joker's ghetto-blaster, compete with Elfman's score for prominence. The power and the glory of film music grandly evoked in the title sequence is essentially soon over — in the grey, everyday working world which follows, Elfman's score is mainly employed to wrap the hero in an aura of grandeur and mystery which is, unfortunately, a few

Iconoclasm in the museum to Prince's music on a ghetto-blaster

sizes too big, like the Batman costume, perhaps because the *Batman* theme was originally meant to complement the overwhelming scale of Gotham City. In any case, the wit, irony and fun in *Batman* is musically connected with the presence of the Joker, who carries his own portable leitmotif in his ghetto-blaster — 'Beautiful Dreamer', played by Hill Bowen and Orchestra, a landmark in department store muzak. When the Joker frightens Vicki Vale in the Flugelheim Museum, the cassette recorder plays Percy Faith's sugar-sweet 'Theme from *A Summer Place'*. Interestingly, this instrumental piece was originally written for an early sixties melodrama, when a version by Percy Faith became a hit — the very definition of easy listening, according to Joseph Lanza (*Elevator Music: A Surreal History of Muzak, Easy Listening and Other Moodsong*, Joseph Lanza).

This reflection of Max Steiner, composer of 'Theme from *A Summer Place'*, appears, to paraphrase a comment by Elfman himself, to have bounced off a series of distorting mirrors. It's supermarket music, a caricature of the dream of beauty and happiness, film music in reduced circumstances, denying the splendour and pathos of Elfman's main title sequence.

Although Elfman integrates 'Beautiful Dreamer' into his score, the result is not as effective as it might be, relying on the sound of the Hill-Bowen strings, which can't compete with Elfman's heroic orchestral sound. There is also a not particularly subtle attempt at irony in the burlesque circus waltz playing during the final show-down with the Joker's gang — as if one were sudd-enly to hear the music from *The Trouble with Harry* (1955, dir. Alfred Hitchcock) at the climax of Hitch-cock's *Vertigo* (1958). The dance element of the Prince songs works better, giving some scenes the flavour of a musical, but the dry, funky sound of these pieces seems to come from a different world to the orchestral music. Although Elfman skilfully worked a motif from the Prince song 'Scandalous' into his score, the over-all acoustic impression is still that the *Batman* sound-track lacks a unifying concept. Elfman remembers his first encounter with the finished product: 'I had the highest expectations when I sat at the première of *Batman*, and it became the low point of my career as a film composer... Batman's music sounded so thin and bloodless' (*Soundtrack!*, 9/1992). So much so, in fact, that Danny never wanted to make an action film again. What had happened?

The curse of the action genre had claimed its usual toll on *Batman*. Once again, the most beautiful musical ideas had been sacrificed for sound effects during the final sound mixing stage, to Elfman's displeasure, 'Sound effects are the bane of film music' (*Sound-track!*, 9/1992). But Elfman often can't leave things alone either — there's hardly an explosion in *Batman* without an accompanying clash of cymbals; the music seems to want to jump to the aid of the pictures the whole time, as if *Batman* had never left the comicbook. (Or as if there was no sound at all on the videotape the composer was working with.) This is the heritage of the Steiners and the Korngolds who did exactly the same — in the thirties and forties. It's precisely in the area of sound technology that the greatest advances have been made in the past two decades — explosions get louder and louder, as critics complain about the acoustic barrage which attacks the audience of films like *Armageddon* (1998, dir. Michael Bay).

Sailing under the false flag of realism, although

they have long been generated with the aid of computers, sound effects are in the process of sending the classic score to the wall, to a certain extent, which is threatening, according to Elfman, to become mere aural wallpaper. The bad sound mixing in *Batman* is, therefore, no simple accident but partly due to the nature of the genre itself. Apparently, multi-million dollar B-movies with an eye to box office takings need an intensified impression of reality, for which the sound effects are these days responsible. Even in a great nihilist work like *Mars Attacks!*, the overriding rule is still that sound effects are serious business.

Back to the sources

'Oh, what a beautiful day': *Pee-Wee's Big Adventure*

Mars *Attacks!* simultaneously evokes and parodies the power of music. The grandmother's (Sylvia Sidney) favourite hillbilly records suddenly become deadly weapons, and the old woman herself is transformed from helpless victim into saviour of humanity when she happens to pull the headphone plug out of the amplifier, filling the old people's home with indescribable, yodelling music. The heads of the Martians explode in disgust — they have heard the voice of America!

The jargon term for music which can be heard by the actors in a film and which can therefore play a direct part in the plot (although the consequences aren't always as devastating as in *Mars Attacks!*) is 'source music', even if the actual source of such music no longer absolutely has to be shown on the screen. So-called 'pit music', which seems to emanate from some invisible orchestra pit, actually comes from the same loudspeakers as the 'source music' — which might lead one to conclude that the distinction between the two is simply a matter of convention. The existence of these different cinematic conventions gives Tim Burton and Danny Elfman something to play with.

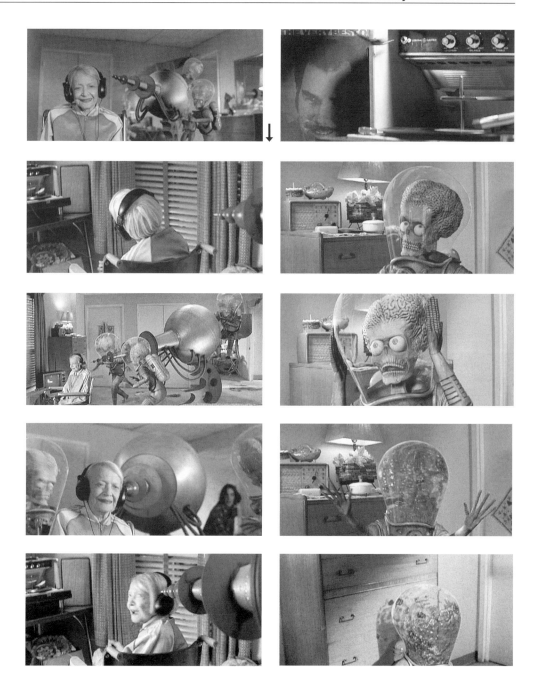

Music as a deadly weapon in *Mars Attacks!*

Burton's characters like to furnish their lives with music. In *Edward Scissorhands*, they paper the walls of their suburban houses with unobtrusive muzak, but music as furniture can be suddenly transformed from an armchair to a torture rack, as in *Batman* or *Mars Attacks!*. Pee-wee gets up in the morning to a song from the record-player, a piece of 'incredibly strange music' that basically consists of a constantly repeated, jubilant melody on strings and the line 'Oh, what a beautiful day' sung in high female voices (and where have we heard that before?). Unlike his later work in *Batman*, Elfman, the Oingo Boingo man, gave *Pee-wee* a little piece of supermarket music which moves from the record-player to the orchestra pit when Pee-wee leaves his room. We hear the sound of the music suddenly become fuller and more direct instead of faint and distant. (Pee-wee also does his own sound effects, accompanying his movements with an ono-matopoeic sing song like a child.)

When Burton speaks of film music as a character, he means that it plays a role — sometimes an impor-tant one, even upstaging the other actors — but it doesn't really set the tone. Like the other essential components of a Tim Burton film, it is in on the act and intricately involved with the rest of the produc-tion, rather than giving authorial, narrative comment from the sidelines. This approach takes into account and approves of that loss of narrative authority which the 'actual' film music, the score, inevitably suffers when it no longer supplies the plurality of musical styles and sources with a unifying framework. As was suggested earlier, the *Batman* title sequence is a vain, nostalgic attempt to evoke the power of precisely that cohesive structure.

Edward Scissorhands is a better demonstration of how subtly one can work within a plurality of musical styles. Southern Californian suburbia as shown here evokes memories of the world both Burton and Elf-man grew up in, and the fact that they had to travel to

Florida to find this world so well-pre-served only confirms that it is an era which belongs firmly to the past. The film music, which doesn't so much want to underscore this world as to live in it, is so in tune with the spirit of the strange non-place and its inhabitants that the conventional distinction bet-ween 'source' and 'pit' music frequently becomes redundant.

Contemporary Hollywood expects stylistic versatility of a film composer — a stylistic versatility, however, which is based on that symphonic idiom which (despite its European background) is regarded as a kind of universal musical language of the emotions. Historical, national, local or ethnic detail is then to be imported as local colour onto this supposedly neutral base. Former jazz and pop musicians (Michael Kamen or Hans Zimmer, for example) are seen as flexible and useful in this sense, and Danny Elfman has proved his ability to play along with his blues-oriented score

for *Midnight Run* (1988, dir. Martin Brest). What is more interesting in *Edward Scissorhands*, for instance, is his almost ethnological exploration of his own childhood, of white American kitsch culture, apparently continuing his earlier work with Oingo Boingo.

Gloomy organ music: Esmeralda in *Edward Scissorhands*

One icon of this kitsch culture is housewives' idol Tom Jones, who plays himself in *Mars Attacks!* ('Hello, I'm Tom Jones'). Joyce, the suburban vamp, who lis-tens to Tom Jones' hits in *Edwards Scissorhands*, is thus associated from the outset with sex. When she appears for the very first time, 'Delilah' is playing in the background somewhere; when Joyce attempts to get Edward drunk, 'the tiger' can be heard singing

'It's not unusual to be loved by anyone'; and when Joyce finally tries to seduce Edward, she switches on a tape deck she has brought along specifically to put herself and Edward in the mood with another Tom Jones song. Esmeralda, the Christian fundamentalist, on the other hand, loses herself in her own delusions (rather like Vincent) with the aid of the gloomy organ chords she coaxes from her living room Wurlitzer — or appears to, for it's all part of Elfman's score, surely one of the first Hollywood soundtracks to make use of the auto-accompaniment feature.

Whether living room organ or department store mambo, it's always Elfman's music which is to be found behind these masks. The remaining 'pit music', commenting on Edward's thoughts and feelings, also fits in wonderfully. Elfman shares a love of (perhaps even a weakness for) Christmas effects with Tim Burton and Max Steiner — harps, vibraphone, pizzicato strings and bells start things ringing, and not just on the *Edward Scissorhands* score. In a sense, this sentimentality finds itself at home here, the jingling of bells in a snowy world, a reminiscence of a fairytale childhood which only exists as a kind of collective memory.

Bibliography

Royal S. Brown: *Overtones and Undertones*, Berkeley/Los Angeles/London, 1994
Joseph Lanza: *Elevator Music: A Surreal History of Muzak, Easy Listening and Other Moodsong*, New York, 1994
Mark Salisbury: *Burton on Burton*, London, 1995
Elisabeth Weis: *The Silent Scream: Alfred Hitchcock's Soundtrack*, London/Totonto, 1982

Details 12/1993
Pluggage on-line magazine
Soundtrack! 9/1992

The Author and His Peers

Tim Burton's work as a film director is characterised by both a highly individual style and a thematic unity one seldom comes across in Hollywood cinema. All his films appear to have been planned down to the smallest detail and executed with virtuoso skill, resulting in a satisfyingly unified whole. Burton's emphasis on the importance of form deserves the title 'art', while the continuity of his themes and deliberate weaving of his own biographical text into the fabric of his movies deserves to be called 'authorship'. And yet, one ought to qualify the image of the sole artistic genius, for otherwise one would be ignoring the contribution of others, who have also left their stamp on his work. To describe Burton's collaborators and colleagues as 'servants of a single artistic personality overshadowing all around' would be a 'romantic transfiguration of the director,' and not a true reflection of 'the realities of film production (apart from a few exceptions)' (*Teamwork in der Traumfabrik — Werkstattgespräche*, Beier, Midding).

Tim Burton would probably have few objections to such a romantic transfiguration of his own persona — that is, after all, part of his strategy. But it would be wrong to forget his team of allies, his close colleagues, some of whom have accompanied him on his creative path for years. Burton can really only claim complete authorship over his earliest work, which was extremely fruitful — many of his current ideas can be found in it. In the case of the full-length feature films, however, other people had a hand in things too. People such as Paul Reubens, the man behind Pee-wee

Herman, for whom *Pee-wee's Big Adventure* was tailored; or David Geffen, responsible for the original idea for *Beetlejuice*; or producer John Peters, who made important changes during the shooting of *Batman*. Furthermore, other colleagues involved in maintaining the films' 'Tim Burton touch' have played crucial roles. 'Touch', incidentally, is an appropriate word here, because a person has to feel an affinity with this 'touch' before they can embark on a project with the director.

Burton was always able to get people interested in his projects, as long as they were on the same wavelength. The chemistry has to be right before he can really work well with others. Burton's films are, in a particular way, the result of successful collaboration, rather than simple delegation and division of labour. The contribution of Danny Elfman's music to the overall impression made by the films has already been discussed, as has the importance of personal empathy in forming the basis of such a working relationship. In this regard, Burton resembles his own heroes, characters who always require complete harmony, almost total identification, in those they choose as friends. To what extent this amounts to self-stylisation and is again part of Burton's biographical project may remain an open question. Shared likes and (perhaps even more importantly) shared dislikes have a great influence on the working relationships of this director, along with a common cultural and sociological background — a feeling of knowing where one comes from and where one doesn't belong any more — that connects him with the key members of his crew.

The Nightmare Before Christmas — A Sweet Dream

The *Nightmare Before Christmas*, Burton's first full-length animated film, is also concerned with origins and a place in life, a place which is perhaps home but is located in the realm of fantasy rather than in reality. The movie is based on an idea Tim

Burton had been carrying around with him for ten years before it was finally realised in 1993. He even drew up some sketches for it during his time at Disney, that highly creative phase which laid the foundations for all his subsequent cinematic work. However, he didn't sign up to the actual film as director, but as producer. Skellington Productions in San Francisco was founded especially for *The Nightmare Before Christmas*, and the young, talented animation specialist Henry Selick was given the director's chair and an opportunity to exercise his skill in stop-motion animation.

The film juggles with the two very different traditions competing for prominence in the film — the American Halloween festival meeting the Christian Christmas myth, horrors of the night juxtaposed with brightly shining lights. Dark and light, good and evil: however perfectly this duality suits Tim Burton's *oeuvre*, it seems surprising perhaps that it found a home at Disney, a film company more inclined to promote family values and tradition. Contrary to expectations, Jeffrey Katzenberg, then head of Disney, was enthusiastic about the project: 'It is different from any film ever made before. It's pioneering work, and this is indeed part of Walt Disney's cinematic heritage', he says in *The Nightmare Before Christmas — The Film, the Art, the Vision*, an official book licensed by Disney. Producer Denise Di Novi recalls: 'Disney was quite involved, but they respected our independence. It was a good experience. Jeff Katzenberg is a clever man — he knows that when one engages a director with a vision, like Tim, it's best not to interfere' (*The Night-mare Before Christmas — The Film, the Art, the Vision*, Frank Thompson).

In retrospect, there were few reasons for Katzenberg to regret his decision. The film received a PG rating (requiring accompaniment by adults) on account

Jack is not familiar with the rituals of Christmas: nice presents

of its somewhat dark tone and the macabre pranks, but that didn't seem to detract from its box office success. The thirty million dollars swallowed up by the project yielded a return of double that amount. The critics, however, were reserved. The American press referred to the 'heartless' story which didn't really touch the audience, and suggested that Danny Elfman's songs weren't catchy enough. Some reviews remarked that the film did not live up to expectations of a festive mood, apparently demanded of Disney productions even by professional critics. With regard to the superb creation of an 'utterly different world... in which not one single recognisable, realistic landscape' is to be seen, as Roger Ebert wrote with approval in the *Chicago Sun-Times*, the critics were, however, in agreement — it was a 'feast for the eyes and the imagination.'

The film tells the comical story of one Jack Skellington, the gaunt king of Halloween Town, who finds himself by chance in Christmas Town amidst the preparations for Christmas, watching the industrious Santa Claus going about his business. Envious of the importance of the Christmas festival and of the respect enjoyed by Santa, Jack decides to kidnap him. He wants to slip into Santa's red coat himself and hand out presents to make the world happy.

Tim Burton fans were not surprised to learn that Jack's distribution of gifts is somewhat unconventional, and chaos is unleashed — the Christmas presents contain cute little shrunken heads and little

Naïveté and childlike innocence: Jack
Skellington

Dracula figures; bats attack baffled children and, to
everyone's consternation, a huge, yellow snake consumes an entire Christmas tree. The film takes visible
pleasure in subverting the customary iconography of
Christmas. It has an alibi at the ready — the main
character, Jack Skellington, doesn't understand the
significance of Christmas because he comes from a
completely different world of signs, where horror is
the order of the day — Halloween. His (foiled) desire
to do good is based on naïvete and a childish innocence delighting in forms, colours and effects but
ignorant of the rituals and references hidden behind
them. This enthusiasm for a childish, pre-linguistic
stage, a time before the semiotic fall from grace when
one is still not conscious of the meaning of things, is a
characteristic of all of Tim Burton's films, for whom —
as we guessed — Jack Skellington is another alter ego.

In *The Nightmare Before Christmas* we once again
come across a common motif of Burton's films — the
outsider, personified here in the character of Sally, an

Burtonesque self-reference: Sally loses her arm

artificial girl created by mad scientist Dr Finklestein. Sally is secretly in love with Jack and, because she is one of the outsiders in Halloween Town, has a highly developed sense of who belongs where. She well knows that Jack doesn't belong in Christmas Town, despite his good intentions, and that he's only fooling himself in trying to be someone he's not. Therefore, *The Nightmare Before Christmas* is also about the existential realisation that you sometimes have to go a very long way before you arrive where you belong.

Burton's colleagues came into their own here. Sally, for instance, is the reult of an idea of scriptwriter Caroline Thompson's, faced with the difficult task of modifying an almost finished script which still didn't quite work properly. The main problem was the lack of an inner motivation for the lead character, and that his intentions were not made explicit enough. So Thompson introduced an extra plot — the relationship between Sally and the demonic scientist, Dr Finklestein. 'Without him, Sally would not have had a past to free herself from,' as Thompson explained (*Screenwriters on Screenwriting*, Joel Engel). And without Sally, one might add, the film would have been virtually deprived of its message, for this clever creature functions as an omniscient commentator who puts the actions of the protagonist, Jack, into perspective. 'It just seems wrong to me', Sally observes, making it easier for us to see through the actions of the main character and lending the film some moral depth.

Many details familiar from other Tim Burton movies make an appearance in *The Nightmare Before Christmas*. Apart from common narrative themes and sets of symbols, the mixture of stop-motion and animation was employed as far back as *Vincent*, Burton's first film. Rick Heinrichs, the animator on *Vincent*, undertook the job of visual consultant for *The Nightmare Before Christmas* — the characteristic effect created when three-dimensional characters are juxtaposed with painted two-dimensional backgrounds comes from him. Of course, everything is much more lavishly done here than in Burton's début film. There was no need to cut corners, and each individual image was animated by hand, meaning that the characters and the moving objects had to be repositioned twenty-four times per second of screen time. There are around 100,000 phases in the seventy-six minute film and, just to give an idea of the scale of the work, the action plays out across 240 sets. Henry Selick and his team gave free rein to their love of detail and there are always new things to be discovered, even after several viewings.

Furthermore, the entire design is in keeping with Burton's predilection for the distorted perspectives of Expressionist silent films, as indispensable in this instance as the stylistic recourse to the Universal horror films of the forties. In the very first scene, the camera hovers over a graveyard similar to those in *Frankenweenie* and, later, *Ed Wood*. While Dr Finklestein clearly refers back to the Frankenstein model, Sally, who loses an arm in a fall, is another instance

Frankenweenie, Ed Wood, The Nightmare Before Christmas, Sleepy Hollow (sketch)

169

Martin Landau and the children in *Ed Wood*; the kidnappers in *The Nightmare Before Christmas*

of pure, Burtonesque self-reference. She is one of a family of characters like Edward Scissorhands and Ed Wood, the director with two left hands. This ongoing creative plundering of his own work goes so far that almost all of the inhabitants of Halloween Town are derived from Burton's singular cabinet of curiosities, from his unmistakable iconography, which is added to and raided again in his later work. The enormous, yellow python who gobbles up a whole, decorated Christmas tree — in *Beetlejuice* it's almost an entire family, for example; or the three rascals who kidnap Santa Claus at Jack Skellington's behest — in *Ed Wood* they knock on Bela Lugosi's door and play trick or treat. Such souvenirs from the realm of Burton's irony conjure up for us an eerily beautiful kind of horror, to the tune of 'Jingle Bells' in a minor key.

Collective originality

If Tim Burton's name is on the box, does that mean he's really involved in it? What part do colleagues such as Henry Selick, director of *The Nightmare Before Christmas*, play in the ideas and the shaping of the film? While his name actually appears in the American rental title (*Tim Burton's The Nightmare Before Christmas*) for advertising reasons, Burton wasn't really involved in the execution of the project, apart from coming up with the initial idea and producing a few drawings. There is, however, consensus among his colleagues about his authorship. 'To a great extent, Tim developed

the story and the concept, he shaped the main characters, provided the tone and the touch', claims Henry
Selick modestly (*The Nightmare Before Christmas —
The Film, the Art, the Vision*, Frank Thompson). And
the film's co-producer, Kathleen Gavin, adds, 'They
not only dug up the treatment [which Burton had pre-
pared for Disney ten years before the film appeared],
but also many of his sketches. If you go into our art
department and look at the walls, you'll find as many
of Tim's original drawings as ones we made ourselves
for the design of the set. So his artistic work back
then was the actual starting point for the shaping of
the film.'

Is it just modesty, or do such assertions express an
understanding of the mechanics of the Hollywood film
market? Is this the result of the fact that famous and
easily recognisable brand names are needed to sell a
product? All those who worked on the project can
point to their achievements beyond their association
with Burton's small circle of collaborators. Colleen
Atwood, the costume designer, is partly responsible
for the Burtonesque slant to *Men in Black*, for instance
(and Danny Elfman's score also helps). Atwood
worked on *Edward Scissorhands*, *Ed Wood* and *Mars
Attacks!*, and also designed the costumes for two films
produced by Denise Di Novi, *Cabin Boy* (1994, dir.
Adam Resnick) and *Little Women* (1994, dir. Gillian
Armstrong). Henry Selick began his career producing
trailers for the music channel MTV. His first animated
short film, *Slow Bob in the Lower Dimensions* (1990),
was highly praised by critics, and he won great
respect for directing animated feature film *James and
the Giant Peach* (1996). Producer Denise Di Novi, one
of Burton's closest friends, produced not only *Edward
Scissorhands*, *Batman Returns* and *Ed Wood*, but also
The Nightmare before Christmas and *James and the
Giant Peach*. In particular, Di Novi had a hand in the
director's more 'personal' works. Even her first work
as a producer — *Heathers* (1989, dir. Michael

Lehmann), a film about teenage angst — displays a great affinity with the world of Burton's imagination. A film showing bourgeois culture as a thin layer of ice which cracks to reveal unimagined depths must have seemed right up Tim Burton's street.

Denise Di Novi began her career as a journalist in Canada, where she then worked for several film production companies, always showing a liking for unusual material. When Tim Burton Productions was founded in 1989, it was Di Novi who managed the company. In 1992, she branched out with her own company, Di Novi Productions, affiliated with Columbia Pictures. *The Nightmare Before Christmas, James and the Giant Peach* and *Cabin Boy* all appeared under this label. Her first film made independently of Tim Burton was a version of Louisa May Alcott's novel *Little Women*, directed by Gillian Armstrong, the all too familiar sounding story of the struggle of a young, aspiring woman writer searching for her place in life. It was promptly nominated for three Oscars — best costume design (Colleen Atwood); best film music (Thomas Newman); and Winona Ryder for best actress.

*The Nightmare Before Christma*s script doctor Caroline Thompson is another member of Burton's unique circle. Thompson got to know him through an agent they had in common, and they hit it off right from the start. Her début novel, *First Born*, was about an aborted foetus in search of its mother, and it made a big impression on Burton. When he showed her a sketch of Edward, with his scissor hands, she had a strong sense of what he was getting at: 'As I grew up in the suburbs and was still coming to terms with this, I immediately understood that this was a clear metaphor for the outsider' (*Screenwriters on Screenwriting*, Joel Engel). Thompson wrote the script of *Edward Scissorhands* — the original plan was for a musical, an idea which was quickly dismissed — in four weeks, a first draft which was later filmed by

Twentieth Century Fox. However, two years passed before the film could actually be made, two years in which Burton made *Beetlejuice* and the first *Batman* film. Thompson once described what they had in common, leaving little room for misinterpretation, as 'a relationship of disgust to the proportions of the world' — the feeling that 'everything is out of joint, physically and mentally' (*Screenwriters on Screenwriting*, Joel Engel). Caroline Thompson was called upon to work on the script for *The Nightmare Before Christmas* at a relatively late stage, when much of the scenery had already been erected in a studio in San Francisco, but the screenplay still left a lot to be desired. Even Danny Elfman's songs (her partner at the time) were ready. Working like lightning for ten days — apparently a speciality of hers — Thompson came up with a script, the rewriting of which doubtless deserves a special place in the history of animated film.

Winona Ryder and Christian Bale in *Little Women*; *James and the Giant Peach*, produced by Denise Di Novi and Tim Burton

The following example indicates how closely the circle works together, and their ability to exercise a certain amount of influence — Denise Di Novi produced two films by director Michael Lehmann, *Heathers* and *Meet the Applegates* (1991). The young director then turned up with a ten-page treatment about the life of Edward D. Wood Jr, written by Larry Karaszewski and Scott Alexander, friends from his student days at the University of Southern California. It was agreed that Michael Lehmann should direct, with Di Novi and Tim Burton producing. At the time, Burton was involved in negotiations with Columbia Pictures over *Mary Reilly*, an adaptation of the Jekyll and Hyde story told from the perspective of the housemaid. Due to pressure of time and Burton's hesitation, Stephen Frears was eventually chosen to direct, and Burton in turn took over direction of *Ed Wood*. The only one who lost out in all this wrangling was Michael Lehmann.

If Burton's name is on the box, does that mean Burton is really inside? It's a notion which isn't quite true, yet counts among the clichés about this film director and artist who has decided to search for mythical stories to describe his own life, and to make a myth of this life; a life, indeed, which like-minded colleagues, admirers and peers choose to identify with themselves.

Filmography

I. SHORT FILMS (DIRECTOR)

VINCENT (1982)

Production: Walt Disney Productions. *Producer:* Rick Heinrichs.

Director: **Tim Burton**. *Screenplay:* **Tim Burton**. *Cinematography:* Victor Abdalov. *Music:* Ken Hilton. *Production Design:* **Tim Burton**. *Technical Director/Animator:* Stephen Chiodo. *Sculpture and Additional Designs:* Rick Heinrichs.

Cast: Vincent Price (Narrator).

Format: B/W. *Running Time:* 6 min.

FRANKENWEENIE (1984)

Production: Walt Disney Productions. *Producer:* Julie Hickson. *Associate Producer:* Rick Heinrichs. *Production Supervisor:* Tom Leetch. *Location Manager:* Rolf Drabo.

Director: **Tim Burton**. *Assistant Director:* Richard Learman. *Screenplay:* Lenny Ripps, from an idea by **Tim Burton**. *Script Supervisor:* Doris Chisholm. *Cinematography:* Thomas E. Ackerman. *Assistant Cinematographer:* William Waldman. *Camera Operator:* Douglas Knapp. *2nd Unit Photography:* Peter Anderson, Rusty Gellert. *Music:* Michael Convertino, David Newman. *Music Supervisor:* Jay Lawton. *Music Editor:* Jack Wadsworth. *Editor:* Ernest Milano. *Assistant Editor:* Marty Stanovich. *Production Sound Mixer:* John Glascock. *Supervising Sound Editor:* Robert Hathaway. *Re-Recording Mixers:* Nick Alphin, Richard Portman, Frank Regula. *Sound Effects Editor:* Joseph Parker. *Production Design:* **Tim Burton**. *Art Direction:* John B. Mansbridge. *Set Decoration:* Roger M. Shook. *Set Costumers:* Sandy Berke Jordan, Milton J. Magnum. *Costume Design:* Jack Sandeen. *Hair Design:* Connie Nichols. *Make-up:* Marvin J. McIntyre, Robert J. Schiffer. *Visual Effects Animation:* Allen Gonzales. *Special Effects:* Haris Metz, Roland Tantin. *Special Electrical Effects:* Ed Angell. *Casting:* Sparky Joe Scully, Bill Shepard.

Cast: Shelley Duvall (Susan Frankenstein), Daniel Stern (Ben Frankenstein), Barret Oliver (Victor Frankenstein), Joseph Maher (Mr Chambers), Roz Braverman (Mrs Epstein), Paul Bartel (Mr Walsh), Domino (Ann Chambers), Jason Hervey (Frank Dale), Paul C. Scott (Mike Anderson), Helen Boll (Mrs Curtis), Bob Herron (Street Player), Donna Hall (Street Player), Sparky (The Dog).

Format: 35mm, B/W. *Running Time:* 27 min.

II. Feature Films (Director)

PEE-WEE'S BIG ADVENTURE (1985)

Production: Warner Bros./Aspen Film Society. *Producers:* Richard Gilbert Abramson, Robert Shapiro. *Executive Producer:* William E. McEuen. *Production Manager:* David Silver. *Location Manager:* Sam Mercer.

Director: **Tim Burton**. *Assistant Director:* Robert P. Cohen. *Screenplay:* Phil Hartman, Paul Reubens, Michael Varhol. *Script Supervisor:* Jan Kemper. *Cinematography:* Victor J. Kemper. *Assistant Cinematographer:* Bill Roe. *Camera Operator:* Robert Thomas. *Music:* Danny Elfman. *Music Supervisor and Arranger:* Steve Bartek. *Music Editor:* Bob Badami. *Editor:* Billy Weber. *Assistant Editors:* Claudia Finkle, John Frazier. *Production Sound Mixer:* Petur Hliddal. *Supervising Sound Editors:* David B. Cohn, Cecelia Hall. *Re-Recording Mixers:* Neil Brody, Scott Brose, David J. Hudson, Terry Porter. *Production Design:* David L. Snyder. *Set Design:* James E. Tocci. *Set Decoration:* Thomas Roysden. *Set Costumers:* Sandy Berke Jordan, Richard Little, Don Vargas. *Costume Design:* Aggie Guerard Rodgers. *Hair Design:* Linda Trainoff, Jeffrey A. Wischnack. *Make-up:* Frank Griffin. *Special Effects Supervisor:* Chuck Gaspar. *Special Effects Co-ordinator:* Joe Day. *Special Visual Effects:* Dream Quest Images. *Animated Effects Supervisor:* Rick Heinrichs. *Title Design:* Anthony Goldschmidt. *Stills:* Peter Sorel. *Casting:* Wally Nicita. *Stunt Co-ordinator:* Paul Baxley.

Soundtrack: 'Burn in Hell' (written by Dee Snider, performed by Twisted Sister); 'Tequila' (written by Chuck Rio, performed by The Champs).

Cast: Paul Reubens (Pee-wee Herman), Elizabeth Daily (Dottie), Mark Holton (Francis), Diane Salinger (Simone), Judd Omen (Mickey), Irving Hellman (Neighbour), Monte Landis (Mario), Damon Martin (Chip), Daryl Roach (Chuck), Bill Cable (Policeman #1), Peter Looney (Policeman #2), Starletta DuPois (Sgt. Hunter), Professor Toru Tanaka (Butler), Ed Herlihy (Mr Buxton), Ralph Seymour (Francis' Accomplice), Lou Cutell (Amazing Larry), Raymond Martino (Gang Member), Erica Yohn (Madam Ruby), Bill W. Richmond (Highway Patrolman), Alice Nunn (Large Marge), Ed Griffith (Trucker), Simmy Bow (Man in Diner), Jon Harris (Andy), Carmen Filpi (Hobo Jack), Jan Hooks (Tina), John Moody (Bus Clerk), John O'Neill (Cowboy #1), Alex Sharp (Cowboy #2), Cassandra Peterson (Biker Mama), Jason Hervey (Kevin Morton), Bob McClurg (Studio Guard), John Paragon (Movie Lot Actor), Susan Barnes (Movie Lot Actress), Zachary Hoffman (Director), Lynne Marie Stewart (Mother Superior), George Sasaki (Japanese Director), Richard Brose (Tarzan), Drew Seward (Kid #1), Brett Fellman (Kid #2), Bob Drew (Fireman), John Gilgreen (Policeman at Pet Shop), Noreen Hennessey (Reporter/Noreen Hennessy), Phil Hartman (Reporter),

Michael Varhol (Photographer), Gilles Savard (Pierre), James Brolin (P.W.), Morgan Fairchild (Dottie), Tony Bill (Terry Hawthorne), Dee Snider (Twisted Sister); *Biker:* Chester Grimes, Luis Contreras, Lonnie Parkinson, Howard Hirdler; *BMX Kids:* David Glasser, Gregory Brown, Mark Everett; *Hobos:* David Rothenberg, Patrick Cranshaw, Sunshine Parker.

Format: 35mm (1:1,85; Panavision), Colour (Technicolor), Dolby Stereo. *Running Time:* 90 min. *Locations:* San Antonio, Texas; Cabazon, Santa Monica, California. *US Release:* 1985.

BEETLEJUICE (1988)

Production: Warner Bros./Geffen Company. *Producers:* Michael Bender, Richard Hashimoto, Larry Wilson. *Associate Producer:* Ralph Meyer. *Production Manager:* Donald Heitzer. *Production Supervisor:* Eric Angelson. *Production Co-ordinator:* Luba Dmytryk. *Location Manager:* Mary F. Galloway.

Director: **Tim Burton**. *Assistant Director:* Bill Scott. *Screenplay:* Michael McDowell, Warren Skaaren. *Story:* Michael McDowell, Larry Wilson. *Script Supervisor:* Carol Sevilla. *Cinematography:* Thomas E. Ackerman. *Assistant Cinematographer:* David L. Parrish. *Camera Operator:* Douglas Knapp. *Music:* Danny Elfman. *Music Editors:* Nancy Fogarty, Robert Badami. *Orchestrator:* Steve Bartek. *Editor:* Jane Kurson. *Assistant Editor:* Louis Benioff. *Production Sound Mixer:* David Ronne. *Supervising Sound Editor:* Richard Anderson. *Re-Recording Mixers:* Gregg Landaker, Steve Maslow, Kevin O'Connell. *Production Design:* Bo Welch. *Art Direction:* Tom Duffield. *Set Design:* Dick McKenzie, John Warnke. *Set Decoration:* Catherine Mann. *Costume Design:* Aggie Guerard Rodgers. *Costume Supervisors:* Linda Henrikson, Chuck Velasco. *Key Hair Supervisor:* Yolanda Toussieng. *Make-up:* Steve LaPorte, Ve Neill. *Visual Effects Photography:* David Stump. *Visual Effects Supervisor:* Alan Munro. *Visual Effects Co-ordinator:* Jacqueline Zietlow. *Visual Effects:* Peter Kuran, Ted Rae, Doug Beswick. *Special Effects Supervisor:* Chuck Gaspar. *Special Effects:* Joe Day, Elmer Hui, William Lee, Tom Mertz, Jeff Wischnack. *Title Design:* Pablo Ferro. *Stills:* Jane O'Neal. *Casting:* Jane Jenkins, Janet Hirshenson. *Stunt Co-ordinator:* Fred Lerner.

Soundtrack: 'Day-O' (written by Lord Burgess and William Attaway, performed by Harry Belafonte); 'Man Smart, Woman Smarter' (written by Norman Span, performed by Harry Belafonte); 'Sweetheart from Venezuela' (written by Fitzroy Alexander and Bob Gordon, performed by Harry Belafonte); 'Jump in the Line (Shake Shake Senora)' (written by Rafael Leon and Raymond Bell, performed by Harry Belafonte); 'I Dream' (by Areza Riandra).

Cast: Alec Baldwin (Adam), Geena Davis (Barbara), Annie McEnroe (Jane Butterfield), Maurice Page (Ernie), Hugo Stanger (Old Bill), Michael Keaton (Betelgeuse), Rachel Mittelman (Little Jane), Catherine O'Hara (Delia), J. Jay Saunders (Moving Man #1), Mark Ettlinger (Moving Man #2), Jeffrey Jones (Charles), Winona Ryder (Lydia), Glenn Shadix (Otho), Patrice Martinez (Receptionist), Cynthia Daly (3-Fingered Typist), Douglas Turner (Char Man), Carmen Filpi (Roadkill Man), Simmy Bow (Janitor), Sylvia Sidney (Juno), Robert Goulet (Maxie Dean), Dick Cavett (Bernard), Susan Kellermann (Grace), Adelle Lutz (Beryl), Gary Jochimsen (Stupid Football Player), Bob Pettersen (Ignorant Football Player), Duane Davis (Very Dumb Football Player), Marie Cheatham (Sarah Dean), Tony Cox (Neitherworld Minister), Jack Angel (Neitherworld Minister/Voice).

Format: 35mm (1:1,85), Colour (Technicolor), Dolby Stereo. *Running Time:* 92 min. *Locations:* Vermont; Culver Studios, Culver City, California. *US Release:* March 1988.

BATMAN (1989)

Production: Warner Bros./Polygram Pictures. *Producers:* Peter Guber, Jon Peters. *Co-Producer:* Chris Kenny. *Executive Producers:* Benjamin Melniker, Michael E. Uslan. *Associate Producer:* Barbara Kalish. *Production Manager:* Pat Harrison. *Production Co-ordinator:* Margaret Adams. *Location Manager:* Chris Brock.

Director: **Tim Burton**. *2nd Unit Director and Photographer:* Peter MacDonald. *Assistant Director:* Derek Cracknell, Melvin Lind, Julian Wall. *Screenplay:* Sam Hamm, Warren Skaaren, from a story by Sam Hamm, based on the 'Batman' character created by Bob Kane. *Script Supervisor:* Cheryl Leigh. *Cinematography:* Roger Pratt. *Assistant Cinematographer:* Nick Schlesinger. *Camera Operators:* John Campbell, Mike Proudfoot. *Model Cameraman:* Peter Talbot. *Music:* Danny Elfman, Prince (Songs). *Conductor/ Music Director:* Shirley Walker. *Orchestrators:* Steve Bartek, Steven Scott Smalley. *Music Supervisor:* Michael Dilbeck. *Music Editors:* Bob Badami, Robin Clarke. *Editor:* Ray Lovejoy. *Assistant Editor:* Simon Harris. *Production Sound Mixer:* Tony Dawe. *Supervising Sound Editor:* Don Sharpe. *Re-Recording Mixer:* Bill Rowe. *Music Scoring Mixer:* Eric Tomlinson. *Production Design:* Anton Furst. *Supervising Art Director:* Les Tomkins. *Art Direction:* Terry Ackland-Snow, Nigel Phelps, Kevin Phipps. *Set Decoration:* Peter Young. *Costume Design:* Bob Ringwood, Linda Henrikson. *Costume Supervisor:* Annie Crawford. *Key Hair Supervisor:* Colin Jamison. *Hair Design:* Janet Jamison, Barry Richardson, Rick Provencano. *Make-up:* Paul Engelen. *Special Visual Effects:* Derek Meddings. *Visual Effects Photography:* Paul Wilson. *Visual Effects Art Director:* Peter Chiang. *Visual Effects Co-ordinator:* Peter Watson. *Special Effects Supervisor:* John Evans. *Special Make-up Effects:* Nick Dudman, Suzy Evans. *Title Design:* Plume Partners. *Storyboards:* David Russell. *Stills:* Murray

Close. *Casting:* Marion Dougherty, Owens Hill. *Stunt Co-ordinator:* Eddie Stacey.

Soundtrack: 'Batdance', 'The Future', 'Vicki Waiting', 'Electric Chair', 'Partyman', 'Trust' (written, produced and performed by Prince); 'Scandalous' (written by Prince with John L. Nelson, produced and performed by Prince); 'Theme From *A Summer Place*' (written by Max Steiner, performed by Percy Faith and his Orchestra); 'Beautiful Dreamer' (written by Stephen Foster, performed by Hill Bowen & Orchestra); 'There'll be a Hot Time in the Old Town Tonight' (written by Joe Hazden, M. Theodore, A. Metz).

Cast: Michael Keaton (Batman/Bruce Wayne), Jack Nicholson (The Joker/Jack Napier), Kim Basinger (Vicki Vale), Pat Hingle (Commissioner Gordon), Robert Wuhl (Alexander Knox), Michael Gough (Alfred Pennyworth), Billy Dee Williams (Harvey Dent), Jack Palance (Carl Grissom), Jerry Hall (Alicia), Tracey Walter (Bob the Goon), Lee Wallace (Mayor Borg), William Hootkins (Lt. Eckhardt), John Sterland (Accountant), Edwin Craig (Ratelli), Joel Cutrara (Crimelord #1), John Dair (Ricorso), Vincent Wong (Crimelord #2), Christopher Fairbank (Nic), George Roth (Eddie), Kate Harper (Anchorwoman), Bruce McGuire (Anchorman), Richard Durden (TV Director), Kit Hollerbach (Becky), Lachelle Carl (TV Technician), Steve Plytas (Doctor), Anthony Wellington (Patrolman at Party), Amir M. Korangy (Wine Steward), Hugo Blick (Young Jack Napier), Charles Roskilly (Young Bruce Wayne), Philip O'Brien (Maître D'), Michael Balfour (Scientist), Liza Ross (Mom), Garrick Hagon (Dad), Adrian Meyers (Jimmy), David Baxt (Dr Wayne), Sharon Holm (Mrs Wayne), Clyde Gatell (Mugger), Jon Soresi (Medic), Sam Douglas (Lawyer), Elliott Stein (Man in Crowd), Denis Lill (Bob the Cartoonist), Paul Michael (Cop), Carl Newman (Movement Double John Lurie); *Goons:* Richard Strange, Carl Chase, Mac MacDonald, George Lane Cooper, Terence Plummer, Philip Tan; *Napier Hoods:* Del Baker, Jazzer Jeyes, Wayne Michaels, Valentino Musetti, Rocky Taylor; *Reporters:* Paul Birchard, Keith Edwards, Leon Herbert.

Format: 35mm (1:1,85), Colour (Technicolor), Dolby. *Running Time:* 126 min. *Locations:* Pinewood Studios, London. *US Release:* 23 June 1989.

EDWARD SCISSORHANDS (1990)

Production: 20th Century Fox. *Producers:* **Tim Burton**, Denise Di Novi. *Executive Producer:* Richard Hashimoto. *Associate Producer:* Caroline Thompson. *Production Co-ordinator:* Mary Cay Hollander. *Location Managers:* Michael J. Burmeister, Robert Maharis.

Director: **Tim Burton**. *Assistant Director:* Jerry Fleck. *Screenplay:* **Tim Burton**, Caroline Thompson. *Story:* **Tim Burton**, Caroline Thompson. *Script Supervisor:* Marilyn Bailey. *Cinematography:* Stefan Czapsky. *Camera Operator:*

Frank Miller. *Steadicam-Operator:* Robert Ulland. *Music:* Danny Elfman. *Orchestrator:* Steve Bartek. *Conductor:* Shirley Walker. *Music Editor:* Bob Badami. *Editor:* Richard Halsey. *Assistant Editor:* Catherine Best. *Production Sound Mixer:* Petur Hliddal. *Supervising Sound Editors:* Richard L. Anderson, David E. Stone. *Re-Recording Mixers:* Stanley Kastner, Steve Maslow. *Music Scoring Mixer:* Shawn Murphy. *Production Design:* Bo Welch. *Art Direction:* Tom Duffield. *Set Design:* Cheryl Carasik, Ann Harris, Rick Heinrichs, Paul M. Sonski. *Set Costumers:* David Davenport, Nancy McArdle. *Costume Design:* Colleen Atwood. *Costume Supervisor:* Ray Summers. *Key Hair Supervisor:* Yolanda Toussieng. *Hair Design:* Irene Aparicio, Rick Provenzano, Liz Spang, Lynda Kyle Walker. *Key Make-up:* Ve Neill. *Make-up:* Fern Buchner, Selena Miller, Matthew W. Mungle, Rick Stratton, Brad Wilder. *Visual Effects Photography:* Peter Kuran. *Special Effects Supervisor:* Michael Wood. *Special Effects Foreman:* Mike Edmonson. *Special Effects:* Michael Arbogast, James Reedy, Gary Schaedler, Brian Wood, David Wood. *Title Design:* Robert Dawson. *Stills:* Zade Rosenthal. *Casting:* Victoria Thomas. *Stunt Co-ordinator:* Glenn R. Wilder.

Soundtrack: 'Blue Hawaii' (composed by Leo Robin and Ralph Rainger); 'It's not Unusual' (composed by Gordon Mills and Les Reed, performed by Tom Jones); 'Delilah' (composed by Les Reed and Barry Mason, performed by Tom Jones); 'With these Hands' (composed by Benny Davis and Abner Silver, performed by Tom Jones).

Cast: Johnny Depp (Edward Scissorhands), Winona Ryder (Kim Boggs), Dianne Wiest (Peg Boggs), Anthony Michael Hall (Jim), Kathy Baker (Joyce Monroe), Robert Oliveri (Kevin Boggs), Conchata Ferrell (Helen), Caroline Aaron (Marge), Dick Anthony Williams (Officer Allen), O-Lan Jones (Esmeralda), Vincent Price (The Inventor), Alan Arkin (Bill Boggs), Susan Blommaert (Tinka), Linda Perri (Cissy), John Davidson (TV Host), Biff Yeager (George), Marti Greenberg (Suzanne), Bryan Larkin (Max), John McMahon (Denny), Victoria Price (TV Newswoman), Stuart Lancaster (Retired Man), Gina Gallagher (Granddaughter), Aaron Lustig (Psychologist), Alan Fudge (Loan Officer), Steven Brill (Dishwasher Man), Peter Palmér (Editor), Andrew B. Clark (Beefy Man), Kelli Crofton (Pink Girl), Linda Jean Hess (Older Woman on TV), Rosalyn Thomson (Young Woman on TV), Lee Ralls (Red-Haired Woman on TV), Eileen Meurer (Teenage Girl on TV), Bea Albano (Rich Widow on TV), Donna Pieroni (Blonde on TV), Ken DeVaul (Policeman #1), Michael Gaughan (Policeman #2), Tricia Lloyd (Teenage Girl), Kathy Dombo (Teen), Rex Fox (Police Sergeant), Sherry Ferguson (Max's Mother), Tabetha Thomas (Little Girl on Bike), Kathy Fleming (Neighbourhood Woman); *Reporter:* Carmen J. Alexander, Marc Macaulay, Brett Rice; *Neighbourhood Extras:* Tammy Boalo, Jackie Carson, Carol Crumrine, Suzanne Chrosniak,

Ellin Dennis, Kathy Fleming, Jalaine Gallion, Miriam Good-speed, Dianne L. Green, Mary Jane Heath, Carol D. Klasek, Laura Nader, Doyle Anderson, Harvey Billman, Michael Brown, Gary Clark, Roland Douville, Russell F. Green, Cecil Hawkins, Jack W. Kapfhamer, Bill Klein, Phil Olson, Joe Sheldon, James Spicer.
Format: 35mm (1:1,85), Colour (DeLuxe), Dolby Stereo. *Running Time:* 100 min. *Locations:* Lakeland, California. *US Release:* 12 December 1990.

BATMAN RETURNS (1992)

Production: Warner Bros. *Producers:* **Tim Burton**, Denise Di Novi. *Line Producers:* Robin D'Arcy, Jenny Fulle. *Co-Producer:* Larry Franco. *Executive Producers:* Peter Guber, Benjamin Melniker, Jon Peters, Michael E. Uslan. *Associate Producers:* Holly Borradaile, Ian Bryce. *Production Manager:* Ian Bryce.
Director: **Tim Burton**. *2nd Unit Directors:* Max Kleven, Billy Weber. *Assistant Director:* David McGiffert. *Screenplay:* Daniel Waters, Wesley Strick (uncredited), based on the 'Batman' character created by Bob Kane. *Story:* Sam Hamm, Daniel Waters. *Script Supervisor:* Janna Stern. *Cinematography:* Stefan Czapsky, Dennis Skotak, George Dodge, James Belkin, Tim Angulo, Garry Waller, Neil Krepela. *Assistant Cinematographer:* Zoran Veselic, Bret Harding, Wade Childress, Drummand S. Edmand, Rich McKay. *Camera Operators:* Rob Hahn, Max Penner. *2nd Unit Photography:* Don Burgess. *Steadicam Operator:* Robert Gorlick. *Music:* Danny Elfman. *Orchestrator:* Steve Bartek. *Conductor:* Jonathan Sheffer. *Editor:* Chris Lebenzon. *Assistant Editor:* Tom Seid. *Production Sound Mixer:* Petur Hliddal. *Supervising Sound Editors:* Richard L. Anderson, David Stone. *Re-Recording Mixers:* Jeffrey L. Haboush, Steve Maslow. *Sound Effects:* John Pospisil. *Production Design:* Bo Welch. *Supervising Art Director:* Tom Duffield. *Art Direction:* Rick Heinrichs, Brent Boates. *Set Design:* Thomas Betts, Nick Navarro, Sally Thornton. *Set Decoration:* Cheryl Carasik. *Set Costumers:* Myron Baker, Eddie Burza, Roberto Carneiro, Marjorie Chan, Jennifer Morrison, Steve Shubin. *Costume Design:* Bob Ringwood, Mary Vogt. *Costume Supervisors:* Oda Groeschel, Norman Burza. *Key Hair Supervisor:* Yolanda Toussieng. *Hair Design:* Joseph Coscia, Norma Lee, Barbara Lorenz, Kim Santantonio. *Make-up Supervisor:* Ve Neill. *Make-up:* Greg Nelson, Brad Wilder, Bob Mills, Ronnie Specter. *Visual Effects Photography:* Gregory L. McMurry, William Powloski. *Visual Effects Supervisor:* Michael Fink, Robert Skotak, Craig Barron, Michael Pangrazio, John Bruno. *Visual Effects Co-ordinator:* Erik Henry. *Special Effects Supervisor:* Chuck Gaspar. *Special Effects Foreman:* Mike Edmonson, Bill Klinger. *Special Effects:* Jan Aaris, Ken Clark, Andy Evans, Dan Gaspar, Elmer Hui, Greg C. Jensen, Karl Nygren, Bruce Robles, Mike Weaver. *Title Design:* Robert Dawson. *Stills:* Zade Rosenthal. *Casting:* Marion Dougherty. *Stunt Co-ordinators:* Charles Croughwell, Max Kleven.
Soundtrack: 'Face to Face' (written by Danny Elfman and Siouxsie & The Banshees, performed by Siouxsie & The Banshees); 'Super Freak' (written by Rick James and Alonzo Miller, orchestrated by Bruce Fowler).
Cast: Michael Keaton (Bruce Wayne/Batman), Danny DeVito (Oswald Cobblepot/Penguin), Michelle Pfeiffer (Selina Kyle/Catwoman), Christopher Walken (Max Shreck), Michael Gough (Alfred Pennyworth), Michael Murphy (Mayor), Cristi Conaway (Ice Princess), Andrew Bryniarski (Chip Shreck), Pat Hingle (Commissioner Gordon), Vincent Schiavelli (Organ Grinder), Steve Witting (Josh), Jan Hooks (Jen), John Strong (Sword Swallower), Rick Zumwalt (Tattooed Strongman), Anna Katerina (Poodle Lady), Gregory Scott Cummins (Acrobat Thug One), Erika Andersch (Knifethrower Dame), Travis McKenna (Fat Clown), Doug Jones (Thin Clown), Branscombe Richmond (Terrifying Clown #1), Paul Reubens (Penguin's Father), Diane Salinger (Penguin's Mother), Stuart Lancaster (Penguin's Doctor), Cal Hoffman (Happy Man), Joan Jurige (Happy Woman), Rosie O'Connor (Adorable Little Girl), Sean Whalen (Paperboy), Erik Onate (Aggressive Reporter), Joey DePinto (Shreck Security Guard), Steven Brill (Gothamite #1), Neal Lerner (Gothamite #2), Ashley Tillman (Gothamite #3), Elizabeth Sanders (Gothamite #4), Henry Kingi (Mugger), Joan Giammarco (Female Victim), Lisa Coles (Volunteer Bimbo), Frank DiElsi (Security #1), Biff Yeager (Security #2), Robert Gossett (TV Anchorman), Adam Drescher (Crowd Member), Debi Mazar (Spice), Nathan Stein (Uncle Sam on Stilts).
Format: 35mm (1:1,85), Colour (Technicolor), Dolby Digital. *Running Time:* 126 min. *Locations:* Hertfordshire; Burbank, California. *US Release:* 19 June 1992.

ED WOOD (1994)

Production: Touchstone Pictures. *Producers:* **Tim Burton**, Denise Di Novi. *Co-Producer:* Michael Flynn. *Executive Producer:* Michael Lehmann. *Production Manager:* Michael Polaire. *Production Co-ordinator:* Susan P. McCarthy. *Location Manager:* Diana Leigh Myers, Elizabeth Matthews.
Director: **Tim Burton**. *Assistant Director:* Mike Topozian. *Screenplay:* Scott Alexander, Larry Karaszewski, from the book *Nightmare of Ecstasy* by Rudolph Grey. *Script Supervisor:* Janna Stern. *Cinematography:* Stefan Czapsky. *Assistant Cinematographer:* Eric Tramp. *Camera Operators:* Phil Carr-Forster, Mark Streapy. *Music and Orchestration:* Howard Shore. *Assistant Editor:* Pam DiFede, Sandra Kaufman. *Production Sound Mixers:* John Kurlander, Keith Grant. *Supervising Sound Editor:* John Nutt. *Sound Effects*

Editors: Ernie Fosselius, Sam Hinkley, Jennifer L. Ware. *Re-Recording Mixers:* David Parker, Richard Schirmer, Michael Semanick. *Production Design:* Tom Duffield. *Art Direction:* Okowita. *Set Design:* Bruce Hill, Chris Nushawg. *Set Decoration:* Cricket Rowland. *Set Costumer:* Stephanie Colin. *Costume Design:* Colleen Atwood. *Costume Supervisors:* Nancy McArdle, Ken Smiley. *Key Hair Supervisor:* Yolanda Toussieng. *Hair Design:* Bridget Cook, Lucia Mace. *Make-up Supervisor:* Ve Neill. *Make-up:* Carrie Angland. *Visual Effects Supervisor:* Paul Boyington. *Special Effects Supervisor:* J. Kevin Pike. *Special Effects Co-ordinator:* Howard Jensen. *Title Design:* Robert Dawson, Paul Boyington. *Casting:* Victoria Thomas. *Stunt Co-ordinator:* John Branagan.

Soundtrack: 'Bunny Hop' (written by Ray Anthony and Leonard Auletti, performed by John Keating); 'Spring Fashion', 'Sweet and Lovely' (written by Alan Braden); 'Kuba Mambo' (written and performed by Perez Prado); 'Que sera sera (Whatever Will Be Will Be)' (written by Jay Livingston and Ray Evans); 'Nautch Dance' (written, arranged and performed by Korla Pandit); 'Grip of the Law' (written by Trevor Duncan); 'Seringa' (written by John Arkell); 'Desolate Village' (written by Bruce Campbell); 'All Creatures of God and King' (arranged by Ralph Vaughan Williams, words by William Draper).

Cast: Johnny Depp (Ed Wood), Martin Landau (Bela Lugosi), Sarah Jessica Parker (Dolores Fuller), Patricia Arquette (Kathy O'Hara), Jeffrey Jones (Criswell), G.D. Spradlin (Reverend Lemon), Vincent D'Onofrio (Orson Welles), Bill Murray (Bunny Breckinridge), Mike Starr (Georgie Weiss), Max Casella (Paul Marco), Brent Hinkley (Conrad Brooks), Lisa Marie (Vampira), George 'The Animal' Steele (Tor Johnson), Juliet Landau (Loretta King), Clive Rosengren (Ed Reynolds), Norman Alden (Cameraman Bill), Leonard Termo (Make-up Man Harry), Ned Bellamy (Dr Tom Mason), Danny Dayton (Soundman), John Ross (Camera Assistant), Bill Cusack (Tony McCoy), Aaron Nelms (Teenage Kid), Biff Yeager (Rude Boss), Joseph R. Gannascoli (Security Guard), Carmen Filpi (Old Crusty Man), Lisa Malkiewicz (Secretary #1), Melora Walters (Secretary #2), Conrad Brooks (Bartender), Don Amendolia (Salesman), Tommy Bertelsen (Tough Boy), Reid Cruickshanks (Stage Guard), Stanley DeSantis (Mr Feldman), Lionel Decker (Executive #1), Edmund L. Shaff (Executive #2), Gene LeBell (Ring Announcer), Jesse Hernandez (Wrestling Opponent), Bobby Slayton (TV Show Host), Gretchen Becker (TV Host's Assistant), John Rice (Conservative Man), Catherine Butterfield (Conservative Wife), Mary Portser (Backer's Wife), King Cotton (Hick Backer), Don Hood (Southern Backer), Frank Echols (Doorman), Matthew B. Barry (Valet), Ralph Monaco (Waiter), Anthony Russell (Busboy), Tommy Bush (Stage Manager), Gregory Walcott (Potential Backer), Charles C. Stevenson Jr (Backer #2), Rance Howard (Old Man McCoy), Vasek Simek (Professor Strowski), Alan Martin (Vampira's Assistant), Salwa Ali (Vampira's Girlfriend), Rodney Kizziah (Vampira's Friend), Korla Pandit (Indian Musician), Hannah Eckstein (Greta Johnson), Luc De Schepper (Karl Johnson), Vinny Argiro (TV Horror Show Director), Patti Tippo (Nurse), Ray Baker (Doctor), Louis Lombardi (Rental House Manager), James Reid Boyce (Theatre Manager), Ben Ryan Ganger (Angry Kid), Ryan Holihan (Frantic Usher), Marc Revivo (High School Punk), Charlie Holliday (Tourist), Adam Drescher (Photographer #1), Ric Mancini (Photographer #2), Daniel Riordan (Pilot/Strapping Young Man), Mickey Cottrell (Hammy Alien), Christopher George Simpson (Organist).

Format: 35mm (1:1,85), B/W, Dolby Digital. *Running Time:* 127 min. *Locations:* Hollywood, California. *US Release:* 28 September 1994.

MARS ATTACKS! (1996)

Production: Warner Bros. *Producers:* **Tim Burton**, Larry Franco. *Executive Producer:* Angela Heald. *Associate Producers:* Paul Deason, Mark S. Miller. *Production Manager:* Paul Deason.

Director: **Tim Burton**. *Assistant Director:* Tom Mack. *Screenplay:* Jonathan Gems, **Tim Burton** (uncredited), based on the trading card series from the Topps Company. *Script Supervisor:* Janna Stern. *Cinematography:* Peter Suschitzky. *Assistant Cinematographer:* Alan Disler, Clyde E. Bryan. *Camera Operators:* Ray De La Motte, Joe Thibo. *Music:* Danny Elfman. *Orchestrations:* Steve Bartek. *Conductor:* Artie Kane. *Music Editors:* Bob Badami, Ellen Segal. *Editor:* Chris Lebenzon. *Assistant Editor:* Tim Amyx. *Production Sound Mixer:* Dennis L. Maitland Sr. *Supervising Sound Editor:* Richard Hymns. *Re-Recording Mixers:* Shawn Murphy, Gary Summers, Randy Thom. *Sound Designer:* Randy Thom. *Sound Effects Editors:* Frank Eulner, Ken Fischer. *Production Design:* Wynn Thomas. *Supervising Art Director:* James Hegedus. *Art Direction:* John Dexter, Hugo Santiago. *Set Design:* Richard Berger. *Set Decoration:* Nancy Haigh, Katherine Lucas. *Martian Character/Spacesuit Design:* MacKinnon & Saunders Ltd. *Set Costumer:* Leslie 'Tinker' Linville. *Costume Design:* Colleen Atwood. *Costume Supervisor:* Sue Moore. *Key Costumer:* Mitchell Kenney. *Key Hair Supervisor:* Candace Neal. *Hair Design:* Norma Lee, Joe Zapata. *Make-up Supervisor:* Valli O'Reilly. *Make-up:* Julie Hewett, Robin Neal, Ve Neill, Bron Roylance, Julie Steffes. *Visual Effects Photography:* Janek Sirrs. *Visual Effects Supervisor:* David Andrews, Michael Fink, James Mitchell, Daniel Radford. *Visual Effects Co-ordinator:* Robert West. *Senior Visual Effects Co-ordinator:* Jill Brooks. *Visual Effects Art Director:* Mark Moore. *Visual Effects Editors:* Bill Kimberlain, Greg Hyman. *Special Effects Supervisor:* Michael Lantieri.

Special Effects Foreman: Donald R. Elliot. *Title Design:* Robert Dawson. *Stills:* Bruce Talamon. *Casting:* Matthew B. Barry, Jeanne McCarthy, Victoria Thomas. *Stunt Co-ordinator:* Joe Dunne.

Soundtrack: 'Escape (The Piña Colada Song)' (written and performed by Rupert Holmes); 'Headstrong' (written by E. Antwi and Filo, performed by Elisabeth Troy-Antwi); 'Indian Love Call' (written by Otto Harbach, Oscar Hammerstein II and Rudolf Friml, performed by Slim Whitman); 'Champagne Fanfare' (written by George Cates); 'Stayin' Alive' (written by Barry Gibb, Maurice Gibb and Robin Gibb, performed by Bee Gees); 'I'm Casting My Lasso Towards The Sky' (written by Jimmy Wakely and Lee White, performed by Slim Whitman); 'It's Not Unusual' (written by Gordon Mills and Les Reed, performed by Tom Jones).

Cast: Jack Nicholson (President Dale/Art Land), Glenn Close (Marsha Dale), Annette Bening (Barbara Land), Pierce Brosnan (Donald Kessler), Danny DeVito (Rude Gambler), Martin Short (Jerry Ross), Sarah Jessica Parker (Nathalie Lake), Michael J. Fox (Jason Stone), Rod Steiger (General Decker), Tom Jones (Himself), Lukas Haas (Richie Norris), Natalie Portman (Taffy Dale), Jim Brown (Byron Williams), Lisa Marie (Martian Girl), Sylvia Sidney (Grandma Norris), Paul Winfield (General Casey), Pam Grier (Louise Williams), Jack Black (Billy Glenn Norris), Janice Rivera (Cindy), Ray J. (Cedric), Brandon Hammond (Neville), Joe Don Baker (Glenn Norris), O-Lan Jones (Sue-Ann Norris), Christina Applegate (Sharona), Brian Haley (Mitch), Jerzy Skolimowski (Dr Zeigler), Timi Prulhiere (Tour Guide), Barbet Schroeder (French President), Chi Hoang Cai (Mr Lee), Tommy Bush (Hillbilly), Joseph Maher (Decorator), Gloria M. Willie Garson (Corporate Guy), John Roselius (GNN Boss), Jonathan Emerson (Newscaster), Tamara 'Ginger' Curry (Hooker), Rebecca Broussard (Hooker), Vinny Argiro (Casino Manager), Steve Valentine (TV Director), Coco Leigh (Female Journalist), Jeffrey King (NASA Technician), Enrique Castillo (Hispanic Colonel), Don Lamoth (Colonel), C. Wayne Owens (Stranger), Joseph Patrick Moynihan (Stranger), Roger Peterson (Colonel), John Finnegan (Speaker of the House), Ed Lambert (Morose Old Guy), John Gray (Incredibly Old Guy), Gregg Daniel (Lab Technician), J. Kenneth Campbell (Doctor), Jeanne Mori (Doctor), Rance Howard (Texan Investor), Richard Assad (Saudi Investor), Velletta Carlson (Elderly Slots Woman), Kevin Mangan (Trailer Lover), Rebeca Silva (Hispanic Woman), Josh Weinstein (Hippie), Julian Barnes (White House Waiter), Ken Thomas (White House Photographer).

Format: 35mm (1:2,35), Colour (Technicolor), Dolby Digital. *Running Time:* 106 min. *Locations:* Buenos Aires; Arizona, Kansas, Las Vegas, Washington DC. *US Release:* 13 December 1996.

SLEEPY HOLLOW (1999)

Production: Mandalay Pictures/Paramount Pictures/Scott Rudin Productions. *Producers:* Scott Rudin, Adam Schroeder. *Co-Producers:* Kevin Yagher, Andrew Kevin Walker. *Executive Producers:* Francis Coppola, Larry J. Franco. *Associate Producer:* Mark Roybal. *Production Manager:* Dusty Symonds.

Director: **Tim Burton**. *2nd Unit Director:* Alan Munro. *Assistant Director:* Christopher Newman. *Screenplay:* Andrew Kevin Walker, Tom Stoppard (uncredited), from the short story 'The Legend of Sleepy Hollow' by Washington Irving. *Story:* Andrew Kevin Walker, Kevin Yagher. *Script Supervisor:* Jayne-Ann Tenggren. *Cinematography:* Emmanuel Lubezki. *Camera Operator:* Patrick Capone. *2nd Unit Photography:* Peter Hannan, Conrad W. Hall. *Music:* Danny Elfman. *Editor:* Chris Lebenzon. *Production Sound Mixer:* Tony Dawe. *Supervising Sound Editor:* Skip Lievsay. *Re-Recording Mixer:* Frank Morrone. *Production Design:* Rick Heinrichs. *Art Direction:* Ken Court, John Dexter, Andrew Nicholson, Leslie Tomkins. *Set Design:* Cosmas A. Demetriou. *Set Decoration:* Peter Young. *Costume Design:* Colleen Atwood. *Hair Design:* Peter Owen. *Make-up:* Peter Owen. *Visual Effects Supervisor:* Jim Mitchell. *Visual Effects Co-ordinator:* Theresa Corrao. *Visual Effects Producer:* Drew Jones. *Special Effects Supervisor:* Joss Williams. *Title Design:* Robert Dawson. *Stills:* Clive Coote. *Casting:* Susie Figgis, Ilene Starger. *Stunt Co-ordinator:* Nick Gillard.

Cast: Johnny Depp (Ichabod Crane), Christina Ricci (Katrina Van Tassel), Casper Van Dien (Brom Van Brunt), Miranda Richardson (Lady Van Tassel), Michael Gambon (Baltus Van Tassel), Marc Pickering (Young Masbath), Christopher Walken (Headless Horseman), Michael Gough (Notary Hardenbrook), Christopher Lee (Burgomaster), Jeffrey Jones (Reverend Steenwyck), Lisa Marie (Lady Crane), Richard Griffiths (Magistrate Phillipse), Ian McDiarmid (Doc Lancaster), Steven Waddington (Killian), Claire Skinner (Beth Killian), Alun Armstrong (High Constable), Mark Spalding (Jonathan Masbath), Jessica Oyelowo (Sarah), Martin Landau (Van Garrett).

Format: 35mm, Colour. *Running Time:* 128 min. *Locations:* London; Surrey; Tarrytown, New York. *US Release:* 19 November 1999.

III. TV Productions (Director)

HANSEL AND GRETEL (1982)

Production: Walt Disney Productions. *Producer:* Julie Hickson. *Director:* **Tim Burton**. *Screenplay:* Julie Hickson. *Cast:* Michael Yama, Jim Ishida. *Format:* 16mm. *Running Time:* 45 min.

THE JAR
(TV SERIES: ALFRED HITCHCOCK PRESENTS) (1984)

Production: NBC-TV/Universal/Alfred Hitchcock Presents. *Producer:* Alan Barnette. *Supervising Producer:* Andrew Mirisch. *Executive Producer:* Christopher Crowe. *Associate Producer:* Daniel Sackheim.
Director: **Tim Burton**. *Assistant Director:* Doug Metzner. *Screenplay:* Michael McDowell, Larry Wilson. *Story:* Ray Bradbury. *Cinematography:* Mario DiLeo. *Music:* Danny Elfman, Steve Bartek. *Music Editor:* Dino A. Moriana. *Editor:* Heather MacDougall. *Sound Editor:* Burness J. Speakman. *Production Design:* Dean Edward Mitzner. *Set Decoration:* Viktoria Hugo. *Costume Design:* Sharon Day.
Cast: Griffin Dunne (Noel), Fiona Lewis (Erica), Laraine Newman (Periwinkle), Stephen Shellen (Justin), Paul Bartel (The Art Critic), Paul Werner (Nazi), Sunshine Parker (Texan), Eileen Barnett (Texan's Wife), Peter D. Risch (Happy Kaufman), Regina Richardson (Female Art Type), Susan Moore (Female Fashion Victim), Nathan LeGrand (Male Fashion Victim), Roy Fegan (Person #1), Leah Kates (Person #2), Lori Lynn Lively (Frail Woman), Jeffrey Steven Kramer (Guest).
Format: Colour. *Running Time:* 24 min.

ALADDIN AND HIS WONDERFUL LAMP
(TV SERIES: FAIRIE TALE THEATRE) (1984)

Production: Platypus Productions/Lion's Gate Films/Showtime. *Producers:* Bridget Terry, Frederic S. Fuchs. *Executive Producer:* Shelley Duvall. *Associate Producer:* Sandra Pearson.
Director: **Tim Burton**. *Screenplay:* Mark Curtiss, Rod Ash. *Lighting Director:* Mark Levin. *Music:* David Newman, Michael Convertino. *Videotape Editor:* Marco Zappia. *Sound Recording and Mixing:* Lee Hirschberg, Chet Himes. *Production Design:* Michael Erler. *Art Direction:* Jane Osman, Richard Greenbaum. *Set Costumer:* Beth Alexander. *Costume Design:* Terry Tam Soon. *Make-up:* Sheryl Leigh Shulman, Ron Figuly. *Special Effects:* Jeff Jackson, Al Kidd. *Video Effects:* Cause & FX. *Video Effects Consultant:* Chuck Cirino. *Technical Director:* Jim Ralston.
Cast: Valerie Bertinelli (Princess Sabrina), Robert Carradine (Aladdin), James Earl Jones (Genie of the Lamp/Genie of the Ring), Leonard Nimoy (Evil Magician), Ray Skarkey (Grand Vizier), Rae Allen (Aladdin's Mother), Joseph Maher (Sultan), Jay Abramowitz (Habibe), Martha Velez (Lady Servant), John Salazar (Servant), Bonnie Jefferies, Sandy Lenz, Marcia Gobel (The Three Green Woman).
Format: Video, Colour. *Running Time:* 47 min.

IV. Other Projects

BEETLEJUICE
(TV SERIES/ANIMATION) (1989-91)

Production: Geffen Film Company/Nelvana Productions/Tim Burton Incorporated. *Distributor:* Warner Bros. TV. *Producers:* Michael Hirsh, Patrick Loubert, Clive A. Smith. *Executive Producers:* **Tim Burton**, David Geffen. *Director:* Alan Bunce, John Halfpenny, Larry Jacobs, Rick Marshall, John van Bruggen. *Assistant Director:* Steve Whitehouse, Gerry Fournier, Jamie Whitney. *Developed by:* **Tim Burton**. *Music:* Danny Elfman (Main Theme). *Editor:* Tedd Anasti, Patsy Cameron, Dan DiStefano, Michael Edens, Eric Lewald, J.D. Smith.
Voices: Stephen Ouimette (Beetlejuice), Alyson Court (Lydia Deitz), Roger Dunn (Charles Deitz), Elizabeth Hanna (Delia Deitz), Tara Charendoff (Clare Brewster/Bertha); *Additional Voices:* Len Carson, Paulina Gillis, Keith Knight, Ron Rubin, Joseph Sherman.
US transmission: 1989-1991 (ABC/FOX).

SINGLES (1992)

Production: Atkinson/Knickerbocker Productions/Warner Bros. *Producers:* Cameron Crowe, Richard Hashimoto. *Director:* Cameron Crowe. *Screenplay:* Cameron Crowe. *Cinematography:* Tak Fujimoto, Ueli Steiger. *Music:* Billy Corgan, Paul Westerberg (Song: 'Drown'). *Editor:* Richard Chew. *Production Sound Mixer:* Art Rochester. *Production Design:* Stephen J. Lineweaver. *Art Direction:* Mark Haack. *Costume Design:* Jane Ruhm.
Cast: Bridget Fonda (Janet Livermore), Campbell Scott (Steve Dunne), Kyra Sedgwick (Linda Powell), Sheila Kelley (Debbie Hunt), Jim True (David Bailey), Matt Dillon (Cliff Poncier), Bill Pullman (Doctor Jamison), Devon Raymond (Ruth), Camilo Gallardo (Luiz), Eric Stoltz (Mime), Jeremy Piven (Doug Hughley), Tom Skerritt (Mayor Weber), **Tim Burton** (Brian), 'Crazy Steve' Olsen (Rob), Bernard Bentley (Spiro) etc.
Format: 35mm (1:1,85), Colour (Technicolor), Dolby. *Running Time:* 99 min. *US Release:* September 1992.

FAMILY DOG
(TV SERIES/ANIMATION) (1993)

Production: Warner Bros./Universal Pictures/Amblin Entertainment/Nelvana Productions. *Producer:* Chuck Richardson. *Executive Producers:* **Tim Burton**, Dennis Klein, Steven Spielberg. *Director:* Chris Buck. *Music:*

Danny Elfman. *Design Consultant:* **Tim Burton**. *Animation Directors:* Robin Budd, Steve Whitehouse.

Voices: Martin Mull (Skip Binsford), Molly Cheek (Bev Binsford), Danny Mann (Family Dog), Zak Huxtable Epstein (Billy Binsford), Cassie Cole (Buffy Binsford). *Running Time:* 30 min. *US Transmission:* 23 June 1993.

THE NIGHTMARE BEFORE CHRISTMAS (1993)

aka Tim Burton's Nightmare Before Christmas
Production: Skellington Productions/Touchstone Pictures. *Producers:* **Tim Burton**, Denise Di Novi. *Co-Producer:* Kathleen Gavin. *Associate Producers:* Danny Elfman, Jill Jacobs, Diane Minter, Philip Lofaro. *Production Manager:* Philip Lofaro. *Production Co-ordinator:* George Young. *Director:* Henry Selick. *Screenplay:* Michael McDowell, Caroline Thompson. *Story (Poem) and Characters:* **Tim Burton**. *Cinematography:* Pete Kozachik. *Lighting Camera Operator:* Eric Swenson. *Music:* Danny Elfman. *Editor:* Stan Webb. *Production Sound Mixer:* Shawn Murphy. *Supervising Sound Editor:* Richard L. Anderson. *Re-Recording Mixers:* Shawn Murphy, Terry Porter, Greg P. Russell. *Production Design:* **Tim Burton**, Denise Di Novi. *Art Direction:* Deane Taylor. *Set Design:* Gregg Olson. *Supervising Animator:* Eric Leighton. *Casting:* Mary Gail Artz, Barbara Cohen.

Voices: Danny Elfman (Jack Skellington [singing]/Barrel), Chris Sarandon (Jack Skellington [speaking]), Catherine O'Hara (Sally/Shock), William Hickey (Dr Finklestein), Glenn Shadix (Mayor), Paul Reubens (Lock), Ken Page (Oogie Boogie), Ed Ivory (Santa), Susan McBride (Big Witch), Debi Durst (Corpse Kid/Corpse Mom/Small Witch), Gregory Proops (Harlequin Demon, Devil, Sax Player), Kerry Katz (Man Under Stairs/Vampire/Corpse Dad), Randy Crenshaw (Mr Hyde/Behemoth/Vampire), Sherwood Ball (Mummy/Vampire), Carmen Twillie (Undersea Gal/Man Under the Stairs), Glenn Walters (Wolfman) etc. *Format:* 35mm (1:1,66), Colour (Technicolor), Dolby Digital. *Running Time:* 76 min. *US Release:* 19 October 1993.

CABIN BOY (1994)

Production: Steve White Productions/Touchstone Pictures. *Producers:* **Tim Burton**, Denise Di Novi. *Director:* Adam Resnick. *Screenplay:* Adam Resnick. *Story:* Chris Elliott, Adam Resnick. *Cinematography:* Steve Yaconelli. *Music:* Steve Bartek. *Editor:* Jon Poll. *Production Sound Mixer:* Edward Tise. *Production Design:* Steven Legler. *Art Direction:* Daniel A. Lomino, Nanci Roberts. *Costume Design:* Colleen Atwood.

Cast: Chris Elliott (Nathaniel Mayweather), Ritch Brinkley (Captain Greybar), James Gammon (Paps), Ricki Lake (Figurehead), Brian Doyle-Murray (Skunk), Brion James (Big Teddy), Melora Walters (Trina), I.M. Hobson (Timmons), Alex Nevil (Thomas), David Sterry (Lance), Bob

Elliott (William Mayweather) etc.
Format: 35mm (1:1,85), Colour, Dolby. *Running Time:* 80 min. *US Release:* January 1994.

BATMAN FOREVER (1995)

Production: Warner Bros. *Producers:* **Tim Burton**, Peter MacGregor-Scott. *Director:* Joel Schumacher. *Screenplay:* Lee Batchler, Janet Scott Batchler, Akiva Goldsman, based on the 'Batman' character created by Bob Kane. *Cinematography:* Stephen Goldblatt. *Music Supervisors:* Jolene Cherry, Leslie Reed. *Editor:* Dennis Virkler. *Production Sound Mixer:* Petur Hliddal. *Production Design:* Barbara Ling. *Art Direction:* Christopher Burian-Mohr, Joseph P. Lucky, Tim Donahue. *Costume Design:* Ingrid Ferrin, Bob Ringwood. *Visual Effects Photography:* Les Bernstein, Bruce Logan. *Special Effects Supervisor:* Thomas L. Fisher. *Special Effects Foreman:* Scott R. Fisher.

Cast: Val Kilmer (Batman/Bruce Wayne), Tommy Lee Jones (Harvey Dent/Two-Face), Jim Carrey (Edward Nygma/The Riddler), Nicole Kidman (Dr Chase Meridian), Chris O'Donnell (Dick Grayson/Robin), Michael Gough (Alfred Pennyworth), Pat Hingle (Commissioner Gordon), Drew Barrymore (Sugar) etc.
Format: 35mm (1:1,85), Colour (Technicolor), Dolby Digital. *Running Time:* 122 min. *US Release:* 16 June 1995.

JAMES AND THE GIANT PEACH (1996)

Production: Walt Disney Productions/Skellington Productions. *Producers:* **Tim Burton**, Denise Di Novi. *Director:* Henry Selick. *Screenplay:* Steve Bloom, Karey Kirkpatrick, Jonathan Roberts, from the story by Roald Dahl. *Cinematography:* Pete Kozachik, Hiro Narita. *Music:* Randy Newman. *Editor:* Stan Webb. *Production Sound Mixer:* Agamemnon Andrianos. *Production Design:* Harley Jessup, **Tim Burton**. *Art Direction:* Kendal Cronkhite, Blake Russell, Lane Smith. *Costume Design:* Julie Slinger. *Animation Supervisor:* Paul Berry.

Voices: Simon Callow (Grasshopper), Richard Dreyfuss (Centipede), Jane Leeves (Ladybug), Joanna Lumley (Aunt Spiker), Miriam Margolyes (The Glowworm/Aunt Sponge), Pete Postlethwaite (Old Man), Susan Sarandon (Spider), Paul Terry (James) etc
Format: 35mm (1:1,85), Colour (Technicolor), Dolby Digital. *Running Time:* 79 min. *US Release:* 12 April 1996.

Filmography: Johannes Roschlau

Bibliography

Abbreviations:

AC = American Cinematographer; BerlZ = Berliner Zeitung; BM = Berliner Morgenpost; Cahiers = Cahiers du Cinéma; Cf = Cinefantastique; EW = Entertainment Weekly; FAZ = Frankfurter Allgemeine Zeitung; FC = Film Comment; fd = film-dienst; F&F = Films & Filming; FR = Frankfurter Rundschau; JPC = Journal of Popular Culture; LA Times = Los Angeles Times; KStA = Kölner Stadt-Anzeiger; MFB = Monthly Film Bulletin; NYT = The New York Times; NZZ = Neue Zürcher Zeitung; RC = Revue du Cinéma; SI = Screen International; S&S = Sight & Sound; StZ = Stuttgarter Zeitung; SZ = Süddeutsche Zeitung; taz = die tageszeitung; TSP = Der Tagesspiegel; VV = The Village Voice

Books by Tim Burton

Tim Burton: *The Melancholy Death of Oyster Boy and Other Stories*, New York, 1997.

On Tim Burton in general

Books: Ken Hanke: *Tim Burton. An Unauthorized Biography of the Filmmaker,* Los Angeles, Renaissance Books, 1999. – Mark Salisbury (Ed): *Burton on Burton,* London, Faber & Faber, 1997. *Articles/Features/Profiles:*
(eng:) D. Adams: Tales from the black side: An interview with Danny Elfman, *Film Score Monthly,* 6/1997, pp20-26. – K. Allman: A little nightmare music, *Details,* 12/1993. – anon: Warner, Burton close to long-term contract, *Variety,* 22.11.93, pp12. – M. Atkinson: Hype dreams, *Movieline,* 3/1993, pp42-46. – D. Ansen: The disembodied director, *Newsweek,* 21.1.91, pp58-60. – C. Brown: Burton's set sights on Corman's X-ray eyes, *SI,* 25.4.97. – Taylor L. White: Tim Burton's bizarre gems, *Cf* [special section], 11/1989, pp64-84 [HANSEL AND GRETEL and ALADDIN AND HIS WONDERFUL LAMP]. – M. Dawidziak: Family dog, *Cf,* 2/1991, pp13. – David Denby: Babes in cinemaland, *Premiere* (USA), 7/1989, pp22-23. – Lawrence French: Puppetmaster Tim Burton, *Cf,* 5/1993, pp34. – K. Hanke: Tim Burton, *Films in Review,* 11-12/1992, pp374-381. – K. Hanke: Tim Burton (Part 2), *Films in Review,* 1-2/1993, pp40-48. – Barry Koltnow: Elfman's split personality, *Los Angeles Daily News,* 31.10.93. – K. Lally: On the cutting edge of movie fantasy, *Film Journal,* 11-12/1990, pp10. – Joe Rhodes: Mad Love: The curious and captivating romance of Tim Burton and Lisa Marie, *Us,* 8/1997. – Ralph Rugoff: Shot through the heart: Director Burton expresses his interest in photography with rare Polaroid camera, *Harper's Bazaar,* 1.9.94, pp418-424. – James Ryan: In the studio with Tim Burton: 'Oyster Boy' and other misfits, *NYT,* 2.11.97. – Mark Salisbury: The fantasy movie world of Tim Burton, *Film Monthly,* 9/1991, pp8-10. – David J. Skal: On the set with Tim Burton, Monster Man, *American Movie Classics Magazine,* 10/1998, pp4, 6. – Frederick C. Szebin/Steve Biodrowski: Tim Burton, *Cf,* 12/1997, pp43. – L.

Tanner: Who's in town, *Films in Review,* 1-2/1991, pp31-34. – T. Taylor: Filmmaker fetishes, *Movieline,* 9/1989, pp8. – Frederick C. Szebin/Steve Biodrowski: Interview with Danny Elfman, *Soundtrack!,* 3/1997, pp4-7. – J. Valot: Tim Burton, *RC,* 5/1990, pp54. **(fr:)** anon: Tim Burton, *24 Images,* 12/1992-1/1993, pp34-35. – Antoine de Baecque: Tim Burton, *Cahiers,* 12/1992, pp84. – Michel Ciment: The Book. Burton on Burton, *Positif,* 3/1997, pp10. – M.A. Guerin: Solitude de Tim Burton, *Trafic,* Summer 1997, pp72-84. – M. Jean: Les effets d'une épidémie, *24 Images,* 12/1995-1/1996, pp32-34. – Thierry Jousse u.a.: L'étrange Noël de Tim Burton, *Cahiers,* 12/1994, pp22-32, 34-37. – Th. Jousse/N. Saada: Mes contes de fees, *Cahiers,* Hors-série, 1992, pp90-91. – I. Katsahnias: Les fictions fatales, *Cahiers,* 10/1989, pp4-9. – I. Katsahnias: Tim Burton: La coupe d'un grand, *Cahiers,* 4/1991, pp39-41. – O. Kohn: Tim Burton [special section], *Positif,* 6/1995, pp14-30. – B. Krohn: Tim Burton, de Disney à Ed Wood, *Cahiers,* 1/1994, pp50-57. – A. Martenez: L'étrange cadeau de Mister Tim, *Vertigo,* 10/1996, pp111-116. – M. Pouquet: Tim Burton. Le jeu singulier de la couleur, *Positif,* 6/1995, pp29-30. – N. Saada: Entretien avec Wesley Strick [writer of BATMAN RETURNS], *Cahiers,* 12/1992, pp64-69. – D. Schweiger: Danny Elfman returns, *Soundtrack!,* 9/1992, pp17-20 [Interview]. – T. Sotinel: Tim Burton, l'enfant à la caméra, *Le Monde,* 17.7.92. – Yann Tobin: Tim Burton [special section], *Positif,* 6/1991, pp16-22. – L. Vachaud/J.P. Coursodon: Tim Burton, *Positif,* 12/1994, pp4-11. **(ger:)** Philipp Berens: Der schwarze Träumer, *Cinema,* 7/1992, pp28. – Daniel Kothenschulte: Ed Wood mit den Scherenhänden. Tim Burtons Filme zwischen Kino und Malerei, *fd,* 14/1995, pp4-9. – Ulrich Lössl: Lieber Gespensterskelette als Micky Maus, *Zitty,* 4/1997, pp52. – Helmut Merschmann: Surfer zwischen den Pop-Welten, *epd Film,* 3/1997, pp24-31. – Helmut Merschmann: *Von Fledermäusen und Muskelmännern – Postmoderne im amerikanischen Mainstream-Kino,* Berlin, 2000 [quoted within: Ökonomie und Maskerade: Tim Burtons 'Batman' - *Verfilmungen,* pp123-148]. – Peter Zander: Meine Frau, das Marsmädchen. Im Grunde seines Wesens ist Regisseur Tim Burton ein großes Kind geblieben, *BerlZ,* 24.2.97.

Interviews
(general and on individual films)

(eng:) David Breskin: *Inner Views — Filmmakers in Conversation,* Boston/London, 1992. – D. Breskin: Tim Burton, *Rolling Stone,* 9.7.92, pp38-42. – T. Charity: Santa claws, *Time Out,* 23.11.94, pp22-23. – D. Edelstein: Mixing BEETLEJUICE, *Rolling Stone,* 2.6.88, pp50-51. – N. Floyd: Space probe, *Time Out,* 19.2.97, pp22. – G. Fuller: Tim Burton & Vincent Price, *Interview,* 12/1990, pp110-113. – G. Indiana: Into the wood, *VV,* 4.10.94, pp58. – G. Smith: Punching holes in reality. Tim Burton, *FC,* 11.12.94, pp52-63. – Caroline Thompson: On Tim Burton, *New Yorker,* 21.3.94, pp196. **(fr:)** H. Béhar: Rencontre avec Tim Burton – Les sortilèges du cinéaste, *Le Monde,* 8.12.94. – H. Béhar: Tim Burton, réalisateur américain, *Le Monde,* 23.6.95. –

T. Bourguignon etc: Tim Burton, *Positif*, 9/1992, pp36-44. – M. Ciment: Un optimisme étrange et perverti, *Positif*, 6/1995, pp17-23. – B. Génin: L'étrange Noël de Monsieur Jack, *Télérama*, 7.12.94, pp32-37. – Michel Henry: 'Il ne faut pas se fier aux apparances', *Positif*, 3/1997, pp8-14. – Th. Jousse/N. Saada: Batman, Edward, Vincent et les autres, *Cahiers*, 12/1992, pp46-50. – Th. Jousse: Entretien avec Tim Burton, N. Saada (Ed): 15 ans de cinéma américain: 1979-1994, pp223-233. **(ger:)** anon: Drogen für die Bosse, *Der Spiegel*, 30/1992, pp172-174. – Michael Althen: Monster statt Märchen. Ein Gespräch mit Tim Burton über die Bürde des Erfolgs, *SZ*, 20.7.92. – Michael Althen/Milan Pavlovic: Monströse Märchen, *Steadycam*, Nr. 22 (1992), pp66-73. – Frank Arnold: Comics als Mythen Amerikas, *TSP*, 21.4.91. – Hasko Baumann: Tassenknüller. Ein Gespräch mit Tim Burton zu MARS ATTACKS!, *Der Schnitt*, 2/1997, p18. – Andreas Conrad: Unter uns Marsianern. Der große Junge: Eine Begegnung mit dem Regisseur Tim Burton, *TSP*, 23.2.97. – Carolin Dendler: Rächer der Enterbten kämpft für Coca-Cola, *Die Welt*, 18.6.92. – Frauke Hanck: Interview mit Tim Burton, *FAZ*, 27.2.97. – Ulrich Lössl: Dieser magische Dilettantismus. Interview mit Tim Burton zu seinem Film ED WOOD, *Zitty*, 14/1995, pp56/57. – Dieter Oßwald: Gebrochene Helden gibt es schon genug, *BerlZ*, 13.7.95. – Marcus Rothe: Die Anspruchslosigkeit mit Träumen füllen, *SZ*, 13.3.97. – Markus Tschiedert: Tim Burton: 'Wir leben auf verrückten Planten', *Moviestar*, 4/1997, pp35-36.

On individual films

VINCENT (1982)

Reviews/other sources: **(eng:)** D. Coleman, *Cf*, 4/1983, pp12. – C. Eller: Buena Vista HV set to release Burton shorts, *Variety*, 3.6.91, p26. – G. Fuller: Tim Burton & Vincent Price, *Interview*, 12/1990, pp110-113. – Taylor L. White: Tim Burton's bizarre gems – VINCENT, *Cf*, 11/1989, p67. **(fr:)** Gilles Ciment, *Positif*, 6/1995, pp27-29. – P. Veck: VINCENT – la magie du noir & blanc retrouvée, *BANC*, 9/1983, pp18-19.

FRANKENWEENIE (1984)

Reviews/other sources: **(eng:)** anon: Edward Scissorhound, *Time*, 20.7.92, p87. – C. Eller: Buena Vista HV set to release Burton shorts, *Variety*, 3.6.91, p26 – M. Mayo. *Cf*, 2/1985, pp4-5. – G.J. Svehla: Midnight Marquee, Summer 1992, pp35-36. – Taylor L. White: Tim Burton's bizarre gems – FRANKENWEENIE, *Cf*, 11/1989, p75. **(fr:)** Gilles Ciment, *Positif*, 6/1995, pp27-29.

PEE-WEE'S BIG ADVENTURE (1985)

Reviews: **(eng:)** anon, *Time*, 26.8.85, p64. – V. Canby, *NYT*, 9.8.85, p15. – N. Floyd, *MFB*, 9.8.87, pp248-249. – P. Kael, *New Yorker*, 4.11.85, pp117-118. – T. Keogh, *Informer*, 4.9.85. – A. Lloyd, *F&F*, 7.7.87, pp36-37. – R. Loynd, *Variety*, 31.7.85, p14. – C. Maude, *Photoplay*, 8/1987, p7. – H. Sklar, *Film Journal*,

9/1985, pp41-42. – J. Summers, *Boxoffice*, 10/1985. **(fr:)** anon, *RC*, 7-8/1987, p29. – M. Chion, *Cahiers*, 7-8/1987, pp56-57. – L. Codelli, *Positif*, 7-8/1986, p36. – C. Godard, *Le Monde*, 9.6.87. – M. Mesnil, *Esprit*, 8-9/1987, pp80-83. – F. Moureau, *Cinéma*, 6/1987, p3. – D. Sauvaget, *RC*, 7-8/1987, p29. – D. Sauvaget, *RC*, Hors-série, 34/1987, pp113-114. – M. Septon, *Grand Angle*, 9/1997, pp37-38.

Other sources: **(eng:)** David Ansen : Hollywood's Silly Season, *Newsweek*, 26.8.85, pp62-64. – L. Borger: New distrib Escurial has first hit with 'unwanted' PEE-WEE, *Variety*, 15.7.87, p30. – B. Bruce: Pee-wee Herman: The homosexual subtext, *Cineaction!*, Summer 1987, pp3-7. – D. Edelstein: Vitamins and irony, *VV*, 20.8.85, p56. – K.E. Johnson: Pee-wee's hermeneutics, *Studies in Popular Culture*, 2/1992, pp51-56. – T. Modleski: The incredible shrinking He(r)man: male regression, the male body, and film, *Differences*, 2/1990, pp55-75. – M. Shapiro: Tim Burton's big adventure, *Cf*, 1/1986, pp38-39. – R.Traviato: In the beginning was the nerd..., *Cinema Papers*, 5/1987, p20. – G.M. Tucker: PEE WEE'S BIG ADVENTURE (Danny Elfman), *Soundtrack!*, The Collector's Quality, 26/1988, pp14-15. – M. Walters: Twee enterprises, *Listener*, 13.8.87. – T.L. White: Tim Burton's bizarre gems – PEE-WEE'S BIG ADVENTURE, *Cf*, 11/1989. – R. Winning: Pee-wee Herman un-mascs our cultural myths about masculinity, *Journal of American Culture*, 2/1988, pp57-63. **(fr:)** R. Bassan: Les comiques actuels sont-ils des monstres? In: *RC*, 10/1987, pp12-13. – P. Kral: L'ère du bric-à-brac, *Positif*, 7-8/1987, pp58-59.

BEETLEJUICE (1988)

Reviews: **(eng:)** anon, *F&F*, 8/1988, pp27-29. – D. Ansen, *Newsweek*, 4.4.88, p72. – R. Corliss, *Time*, 11.4.88, p69. – K. Counts, *Hollywood Reporter*, 28.3.88. – D. Denby, *New York Magazine*, 2.5.88, pp91-93. – D. Edelstein, *VV*, 5.4.88, p72. – J. Galbraith, *Variety*, 30.3.88, p12. – P. Kael, *New Yorker*, 18.4.88, p119. – N. Kolomitz, *Film Journal*, 4/1988, p22. – J. Kozak, *Boxoffice*, 6/1988. – J. Maslin, *NYT*, 30.3.88. – P. Moore, *New Statesman & Society*, 26.8.88, pp42-43. – K. Newman, *MFB*, 8/1988, pp227-228. – R.J. Pardin, *Films in Review*, 8-9/1988, pp415-416. – D. Quinlan, *Photoplay*, 9/1988, pp32-35. – D. Shipman, *Contemporary Review*, 4/1989, pp209-212. – M. Walters, *Listener*, 11.8.88, p32. **(fr:)** Y. Alion, *RC*, Hors-série, 35/1988, p19. – R.-C. Bérubé, *Séquences*, 9/1988, pp102-103. – A. Garsault, *Positif*, 2/1989, pp61-63. – M. Girard, *Séquences*, 9/1988, pp102-103. – M.-C. Loiselle, *24 Images*, Autumn 1988, p106. – N. Saada, *Cahiers*, 12/1988, pp50-51. – J. Siclier, *Le Monde*, 27.12.88. **(ger:)** Ambo, *StZ*, 11.11.88. – anon, *Rheinischer Merkur*, 21.10.88. – Helmut W. Banz, *KStA*, 12.11.88. – gil, *StZ*, 12.11.88, p15. – pem, *BM*, 10.11.88. – H.G. Pflaum, *SZ*, 10.11.88, p15. – rue., *NZZ*, 8.12.88, p34. – *Cinema*, 11/1988, pp12-16. – Claudius Seidl, *Die Zeit*, 18.11.88, p61. – Rolf Selas, *Rheinische Post*, 11.11.88. – Anke Sterneborg, *TSP*, 10.11.88. – Ralph Umard, *tip*, 24/1998. – Rudolf Worschech, *epd Film*, 11/1988, p33.

Other sources: **(eng:)** V. Canby: BEETLEJUICE is pap for the eyes, *NYT*, 8.5.88, p19. – F.P. Clarke: BEETLEJUICE, *Cf*, 2-3/1988, p21. – D. Fischer: The making of BEETLEJUICE – Special visual effects, *Cf*, 11/1989, p79. – P.J. Lehti: 'The Whales of August': Alan Price, *Soundtrack!*, The Collector's Quarterly, 27/1988, pp17-18. – J.D. Shannon: Cheap and cheesy and off-the-cuff: The effects of BEETLEJUICE, *Cinefex*, 5/1988, pp4-33. – D. Turner: Storyboarding key to BEETLEJUICE effects, *AC*, 12/1988, pp28-34. – G. Turner: Eccentric is the word for BEETLEJUICE, *AC*, 4/1988, pp74-78. – T.L. White: The making of Tim Burton's BEETLEJUICE & and his other bizarre gems, *Cf*, 11/1989, pp64-84. **(ger:)** Scott Orlin: Höllische Tricks, *Cinema*, 11/1988, pp16-18. – Dietmar Schmidt: BEETLEJUICE, *Enzyklopädie des phantastischen Films* (*Loseblattwerk*, 12. Erg. Lief., Oct. 1989). – Frank Schnelle: Winona [Ryder] forever, *Steadycam*, Nr. 30 (1995), pp32-37.

BATMAN (1989)

Tie-in books: Craig Shaw Gardner: *Batman*, München, 1989. – John Marriot: *Batman: Der offizielle Bildband zum Film*, München, 1989.

Reviews: **(eng:)** P. Baumann, *Commonweal*, 22.9.89, pp502-503. – R. Bishop, *Cinema Papers*, 9/1989, p60. – V. Canby, *NYT*, 23.6.89. – R. Corliss, Time, 19.6.89, pp60-61. – D. Denby, *New York Magazine*, 17.7.89, pp45-46. – R. Ebert, *Chicago Sun-Times*, 23.6.89. – K. Hanke, *Films in Review*, 10/1989, pp480-482. – J. Hoberman, *VV*, 4.7.89, p69. – T. Hutchinson, *Film Monthly*, 9/1989, p21. – K. Johns, *Film Monthly*, 8/1989, pp14-16. – P. Kael, *New Yorker*, 10.7.89, pp83-85. – F. Kaspersen, *Kosmorama*, Winter 1989, p46. – P. Kauffmann, *New Republic*, 31.7.89, pp24-25. – P. Klawans, *Nation*, 17.7.89, pp98-101. – J. Kroll, *Newsweek*, 26.6.89, pp72-73. – K. Lally, *Film Journal*, 7/1989, pp9-10. – J. McBride, *Variety*, 14.6.89, p7. – T. Matthews, *Boxoffice*, 9/1989, pp37, 45. – K. Newman, *MFB*, 9/1989, pp268-269. – R. Pennington, *Hollywood Reporter*, 15.6.89, pp4, 22. – P. Rainer, *American Film*, 11/1989, pp70-72. – J. Simon, *National Review*, 18.8.89, p46. – M. Steff, *National Review*, 15.9.89, pp55-57. – M. Walters, *Listener*, 10.8.89, pp30-31. – T.L. White, *Cf*, 5/1989, pp8-9. – B. Zehme, *Rolling Stone*, 29.6.89, pp38-42. **(fr:)** R.-C. Bérubé, *Séquences*, pp95-96. – G. Lenne, *RC*, 10/1989, pp19-20. – Y. Lafontaine, *24 Images*, Autumn 1989, pp96-97. – F. Ramasse, *Positif*, 11/1989, pp69-72. – P. Ross, *RC*, Hors-série, 36/1989, p22. **(ger:)** Patrick Bahners, *FAZ*, 31.10.89. – Inge Bongers, *Volksblatt Berlin*, 27.10.89. – H. Cadera, *Filmfaust*, 10.11.89. – Thierry Chervel, *taz*, 26.10.89. – Brigitte Desalm, *KStA*, 28.10.89. – dlw., *NZZ*, 26.10.89, pp47-48. – Barry Graves, *tip*, 22/1989. – R. James, *Film und Fernsehen*, 9/1989, pp40-41. – Andreas Kilb, *Die Zeit*, 27.10.89, p69. – Thomas Klingenmair, *StZ*, 28.10.89, p41. – Michael Kölz, *FR*, 27.10.89, p20. – M. Langes, *Die Welt*, 23.10.89, p17. – M. Matussek, *Der Spiegel*, 23.10.89, pp248-254. – Peter E. Müller, *BM*, 25.10.89. – Thorsten Pietsch, *taz*, 3.11.89. – Angelika Ohland, *Deutsches Allgemeines Sonntagsblatt*, 27.10.89, p23. – Hans Günther Pflaum, *SZ*,

26.10.89, p49. – Bernhard Praschl, *Presse*, 28.10.89. – Alfred Starkmann, *Die Welt*, 21.6.89, p22. – Henry Steinhau, Wahrheit, 27.10.89. – Anke Sterneborg, *TSP*, 25.10.89. – Ulrich von Thüna, *epd Film*, 10/1989, pp36-37.

Other sources: **(eng:)** anon: Kids banned from Batman: WB files new appeal, *Variety*, 27.9.89, p15. – anon: Tribute: BATMAN's architect, *People*, 9.12.91, p55. – R. Bateman: BATMAN in his belfry, *American Film*, 4/1989, p8. – B. Barol: Batmania, *Newsweek*, 26.6.89, pp70-74. – P. Benson: Bat*angst* is basic black, *LA Times*, 23.6.89. – F.P. Clarke: BATMAN: Caped crusader casting calamity, *Cf*, 19/1989, p14. – P. Cohl: BATMAN exclusive preview!, *Film Threat* 18/1989, pp20-23. – L.L. Cohn: BATMAN – A 10-year journey for Uslan and Melniker, *Variety*, 7.6.89, p5. – G. DeBona: The canon and cultural studies: Culture and anarchy in Gotham City, *Journal of Film and Video*, 1-2/1997, pp52-65. – R. Corliss/E. Dutka: The caped crusader flies again, *Time*, 19.6.89, pp60-62. – J.R. Dequindre: A blackout hits Gotham?, *Film Threat*, 8/1992, p27. – Hilary DeVries: BATMAN battles for big money, *NYT*, 5.2.89, p11. – T. Doherty: BATMAN, *Cf*, 3/1990, pp42-43. – D. Gire: Rating the bat, *Cf*, 1-2/1989, pp56-57. – M. Goldberg: Rock & Roll: Prince scores BATMAN film, *Rolling Stone*, 29.6.89, p21. – P. Goldberger: Celtics notebook: New York as setting and as star, *NYT*, 11.7.89, p13. – P. Greco: Planet design, *Interview*, 6/1991, p34. – A. Harmetz: The Joker is wild, *NYT*, 18.6.89, p16. – A. Jones: BATMAN, *Cf*, 11/1989, pp48-62. – J. Kroll: Return to Gotham City, *Newsweek*, 23.1.89, pp68-69. – John Lahr: Tim Burton's dark knight, *Fame*, 8/1989. – R.Magid: BATMAN voodoo mostly from Britain, *AC*, 12/1989, pp58-60. – T. Minsky: Batguy, *Premiere* (USA), 7/1989, pp48-51. – E. Mitchell: Sam Hamm's BATMAN plan, *Rolling Stone*, 12/1988, p33. – Joe Morgenstern: Tim Burton, Batman and the Joker, *NYT*, 9.4.89, pp44-46. – A. Nightingale: Batman prowls a Gotham drawn from the absurd, *NYT*, 18.6.89, p1. – P.L. Parmalee: Rethinking Utopia: From METROPOLIS to BATMAN, *Rethinking Marxism*, 2/1991, pp79-91. – J. Rainone: BATMAN: The third incarnation, *Metro*, Spring 1989, pp7-9. – P. Rebello: Sam Hamm – A profile of the hot new screenwriter who launched the Dark Knight's boxoffice torpedo, *Cf*, 11/1989, pp43-47. – H.A. Rodman: They shoot comicbooks, don't they?, *American Film*, 5/1989, pp34-39. – D. Roland: Danny Elfman on scoring BATMAN, *Premiere* (USA), 4/1989, pp7-8. – J. Rosenbaum: Are you having fun, *S&S*, Spring 1990, pp96-97. – A. Ross: Ballots, bullets, or batmen: Can cultural studies do the right thing?, *Screen*, Spring 1990, pp26-44. – Dan Scapperott: Bat-History 101, *Cf*, 11/1989. – T. Sciacca: Batman: The comic connection, *Variety*, 28.6.89, pp6-7. – J.D. Shannon: A dark and stormy knight, *Cinefex*, 2/1990, pp4-33. – J. Silverthorne: The cave, *Artforum*, 9/1989, pp12-14. – A. Thompson: After BATMAN: Anatomy of a deal, *Los Angeles Weekly*, 23.11.90. – A. White: Prince of the city, *FC*, 11-12/1989, pp76-78 [on the Prince videos 'Batdance' and 'Partyman']. **(fr:)** I. Katsahnias/B. Krohn: Vampire. Batmania en neuf temps, *Cahiers*, 9/1989, pp14-21. – G. Lebouc: BATMAN, *Grand Angle*, 9/1989, pp13-14. – M.

Mesnil: BATMAN et Batmania, *Esprit*, 2/1990, pp41-48. – N. Saada: Prince: BATMAN, *Cahiers*, Hors-série, 1995, p127. – J. Zimmer: Bat's back, *RC*, 12/1988. **(ger:)** anon: Die Rückkehr des dunklen Ritters, *Der Spiegel*, 27/1989, p156. – anon: 'Was sie alles so denken', *Die Welt*, 23.10.89 [Statements from Burton and Keaton]. – Brigitte Desalm: Badman, Madman. Jack Nicholson, *Steadycam*, Nr. 13 (3/1989), pp40-47. – Michael Fuchs: Batman schwebt über uns, *Die Welt*, 30.9.89. – Carsten Herz: Die Rückkehr des Superhelden, *Volksblatt Berlin*, 25.8.89. – Milan Pavlovic: Amerikanische Geschichten, *Steadycam*, Nr. 13 (3/1989), pp12-22. – Milan Pavlovic: Unter Wasser stirbt man nicht. Ein Gespräch mit James Cameron, *Steadycam*, Nr. 14 (4/1989), pp50-54. – Milan Pavlovic: In Zahlen, *Steadycam*, Nr. 14 (4/1989), pp5-9 [Box office analysis of BATMAN]. – Harald Pusch: BATMAN, *Enzyklopädie des phantastischen Films* (*Loseblattwerk*, 13. Erg. Lief., Dez. 1989). – Rüdiger Scharf: BATMAN's Berliner Kinostart: Begeisterung der Fans in Maßen, *BM*, 27.10.89. – Georg Seeßlen: Der Triumph des Zeichens über die Begierde, in: *Clint Eastwood trifft Federico Fellini. Essays zum Kino*, Berlin 1996, pp168-181. – Thomas Steiger: Ronald Reagan's Fledermaus – Comic-Held, Kulturerbe und Psychopath, *TSP*, 12.7.92. – Jörg Stray: Eine Fledermaus wird Mode-Hit, *BM*, 11.8.89. – Silke Svatunek etc: BATMAN, *Cinema*, 10/1989, pp11-25. – Christoph Terhechte: Tee mit dem Wachpersonal – In Frankreich ist der 'Film zum Hemd' ein Flop, *taz*, 26.10.89.

EDWARD SCISSORHANDS (1990)

Reviews **(eng:)** R. Aleva, *Commonweal*, 8.2.91, pp100-101. – anon, *SI*, 8.12.90, p10. – D. Ansen, *Newsweek*, 10.12.90, p87. – A. Billson, *New Statesman & Society*, 26.7.91, p32. – P. Biodrowski, *Cf*, 4/1991, p5. – D. Byrge, *Hollywood Reporter*, 3.12.90. – R. Corliss, *Time*, 10.12.90, p87. – D., *Variety*, 10.12.91, p84. – D. Denby, *New York Magazine*, 10.12.90, p84. – R. Ebert, *Chicago Sun-Times*, 14.12.90. – A. Frank, *Film Monthly*, 8/1991, pp20-21. – J. Gelmis, *Newsday*, 2.12.90. – J. Hoberman, *VV*, 11.12.90, p69. – P. Kael, *New Yorker*, 17.12.90, pp115-121. – P. Klawans, *Nation*, 7.1.91, pp22-24. – C.D. Leayman, *Cf*, 6/1991, pp47-48. – J. Maslin, *NYT*, 7.12.90. – M. Meisel, *Film Journal*, 1/1991, pp43-44. – M. Moss, *Boxoffice*, 1/1991. – P. Strick, *S&S*, 7/1991, pp42-43. – G.J. Svehla, *Midnight Marquee*, Summer 1991, pp39-40. – P. Travers, *Rolling Stone*, 10.1.91, pp53-54. – J.M. Welsh, *Films in Review*, 3-4/1991, p110. **(fr:)** anon, *Cinéma*, 2.4.91, p41. – M. Elia, *Séquences*, 3/1991, pp78-79. – G. Grugeau, *24 Images*, 1-2/1991, pp59-60. – T. Jousse, *Cahiers*, Hors-série, 1993, p52. – I. Katsahnias/A. de Baecque, *Cahiers*, 4/1991, pp32-37, 39-41. – Nopere, *Grand Angle*, 4-5/1991, pp17-18. – Ruet, *Cinéma*, 4/1991, p41. – J. Siclier, *Le Monde*, 17.4.91. – J. Valot, *RC*, 4/1991, p40, and Hors-série, 39/1991, p39. **(ger:)** anon, *Max*, 4/1991. – Christof Boy, *taz*, 18.4.91. – Klaus Dahm, *Cinema*, 4/1991, pp34-37. – Brigitte Desalm, *KStA*, 20.4.91. – Brigitte Desalm, *Steadycam*, Nr. 18 (1991), pp72-73. – *Der Schnitt*, 1/1996, pp4f. – Eberhard von Elterlein, *BM*, 18.4.91. – Barry Graves, *tip*, 8/1991.

– Ronald Glomb, *Volksblatt*, 18.4.91. – Fritz Göttler, *SZ*, 27.4.91. – Angelika Kettelhack, *BerlZ*, 22.4.91. – R Ko, *StZ*, 19.4.91. – Peter Körte, *FR*, 19.4.91. – Jochen Metzner, *TSP*, 18.4.91. – ric., *FAZ*, 4.5.91. – Ritz, *NZZ*, 26.4.91. – Frank Schnelle, *epd Film*, 4/1991, p36. – Reinhard Tschapke, *Die Welt*, 18.4.91. *Other sources:* **(eng:)** Nina J. Easton: For Tim Burton, his one's personal, *LA Times*, 12.8.90. – P. Gaydos: On location: EDWARD SCISSORHANDS, *Hollywood Reporter*, 31.7.90. – A. Jones: Tim Burton's EDWARD SCISSORHANDS, *Cf*, 5/1994, pp12-19. – P.R. Johnson: 'I'm not finished!' – The evolving male in the modern fantasy film, *Midnight Marquee*, Winter 1994, pp45-49. – K. Lally: On the cutting edge of movie fantasy, *Film Journal*, 11-12.90, p10. – C.D. Leayman: Filming Edward's fantasy castle, *Cf*, 6/1991, p47. – R. Marich: Fox positions SCISSORHANDS, *Hollywood Reporter*, 14.11.90, p9. – C. Maude: Buried pleasure, *Time Out*, 24.7.91, p27. – F. Rose: Tim cuts up, *Premiere* (USA), 1/1991, pp96-102. – M. Salisbury: Caroline Thompson. Writer – Director, *Empire*, 3/1995, p48. – L. H. Smith: Ma, no hands, or Tim Burton's latest feat, *NYT*, 26.8.90, p18. – Starburst, 7/1991, pp30-39 [Burton on writing the screenplay]. – Louise Tanner: Who's in town, *Films in Review*, 1-2/1991, pp31-34. **(fr:)** A. de Baecque: L'Amérique sous les fers, *Cahiers*, 4/1991, pp36-37. – T. Bourguignon: Edward l'ermite, *Positif*, 6/1991, pp8-11. – Garsault: Du conte et du mythe, *Positif*, 6/1991, pp12-15. **(ger:)** Thomas F. Roth etc: EDWARD SCISSORHANDS, *Enzyklopädie des phantastischen Films* (*Loseblattwerk*, 22. Erg. Lief., Dec. 1991).

BATMAN RETURNS (1992)

Tie-in books: Craig Shaw Gardner: Batmans Rückkehr, München, 1992.

Reviews: **(eng:)** R. Alleva, *Commonweal*, 14.8.92, pp28-29. – G., *Time Out*, 8.7.92, p58. – D. Ansen, *Newsweek*, 22.6.92, pp50-51. – B., *New Statesman & Society*, 10.7.92, pp31-32. – R.A. Blake, *America*, 15.8.92, p89. – B. Cramer, *Films in Review*, 9-10/1992, pp337-339. – D. Denby, *New York Magazine*, 13.7.92, pp63-64. – T. Doherty, *Cf*, 2-3/1992, pp8-9. – R. Ebert, *Chicago Sun-Times*, 19.6.92. – M. Gray, *Film Monthly*, 9/1992, pp12-13. – J. Hoberman, *VV*, 30.6.92, p57. – C. James, *NYT*, 28.6.92, p11. – P. Kauffmann, *New Republic*, 27.7.92, pp46-47. – P. Klawans, *Nation*, 13.7.92, pp64-65. – K. Lally, *Film Journal*, 7/1992, p33. – R.-M. Loughnane, *Metro*, Spring 1993, pp18-22. – J. Maslin, *NYT*, 19.6.92, p1. – T. McCarthy, *Variety*, 15.6.92, p56. – R. Meyers, *Armchair Detective*, 1/1993, pp64-66. – K. Newman, *S&S*, 8/1992, pp48-49. – T. Rafferty, *New Yorker*, 29.6.92, pp71-72. – F. Schruers, *Premiere* (USA), 7/1992, pp56-64. – J. Schwager, *Boxoffice*, 8-9/1992. – J. Simon, *National Review*, 8/1992, pp48-49. – G.J. Svehla, *Midnight Marquee*, Summer 1993, pp87-89. – P. Travers, *Rolling Stone*, 9.7.92, p109. – A.J. Vanek, *Film Threat*, 10/1992, pp54-55. – T.L. White, *Cf*, 1/1992, pp8-11. **(fr:)** A. de Baecque, *Cahiers*, 7-8/1992, pp76-79. – R. Bassan, *RC*, 7-8/1992, pp24-25. – T. Bourguignon, *Positif*, 9/1992, pp37-39. – J.-M. Frodon, *Le Monde*, 17.7.92. – M.

Girard, *Séquences*, 9/1992, pp61-62. **(ger:)** Michael Althen, *SZ*, 17.7.92. – Carl Andersen, *Neues Deutschland*, 16.7.92. – Patrick Bahners, *FAZ*, 22.7.92. – Philipp Berens, *Cinema*, 7/1992, pp20-26. – Thierry Chervel, *taz*, 16.7.92. – Brigitte Desalm, *KStA*, 18.7.92. – Brigitte Desalm, *Steadycam*, Nr. 22 (1992), p67. – dlw., *NZZ*, 23.7.92. – Franz Everschor, *fd*, 21.7.92, pp22-23. – Rupert Koppold, *StZ*, 15.7.92. – Christiane Kruttschnitt, *Stern*, 16.7.92. – Harald Martenstein, *TSP*, 17.7.92. – Peter E. Müller, *BM*, 16.7.92. – Fritz Murr, *FR*, 17.7.92. – Rainer Nolden, *Die Welt*, 15.7.92. – Harry Rowohlt, *Die Zeit*, 24.7.92. – Günter Sobe, *BerlZ*, 23.7.92. – Christoph Terhechte, *tip*, 15/1992. – Claudia Wefel, *epd Film*, 8/1992, p36.

Other sources: **(eng:)** D. Ansen: How to make the suits nervous but happy, *Newsweek*, 22.6.92, p51. – P. Beard: Cape of good hype, *Modern Review*, Summer 1992, p30. – P.M. Bernardo: Recycling victims and villains in BATMAN RETURNS, *Literature/Film Quarterly*, 1/1994, pp16-20. – J. Compeau: Flapping over old ground, *Film Threat*, 8/1992, p34. – R. Corliss etc: The battier the better, *Time*, 22.6.92, pp69-71. – P. Dayle: Sets appeal: Designing BATMAN RETURNS, *EW*, 19.6.92, pp24. – P. Dayle: Unhappy RETURNS batlash, *EW*, 31.7.92. – J.R. Dequindre/J. Compeau: A bat attitude, *Film Threat*, 8/1992, pp24-26. – R. Ebert: The batbrain director, *Los Angeles Daily News*, 21.6.92, p3. – C. Eller: Burton to do BATMAN 2, Keaton up in air, *Variety*, 14.1.91, p21. – P. Farrell: Bat beat, *Scarlet Street*, Summer 1992, pp19-20. – P. Farrell/D. Sullivan: Bat beat, *Scarlet Street*, Winter 1992, pp22-23. – L. Grobel: Little big man, *Movieline*, 7/1992, pp26-31. – M. Lipsky: Letters: BATMAN RETURNS, *NYT*, 12.7.92, p4. – R. Magid: Back to Gotham: BATMAN RETURNS, *AC*, 7/1992, pp34-51 [Interview with cinematographer Czapsky]. – P. Orr: The anoedipal Mythos of Batman and Catwoman, *JPC*, 4/1994, pp169-182. – J. Pendleton: BATMAN RETURNS merchandise not going through the roof, *Variety*, 3.8.92, p58. – J. Pendleton: Manic bat-marketing underway, *Variety*, 20.4.92, p3. – Cory A. Reed: Batman returns: from the comic(s) to the grotesque, *Post Script*, Summer 1995, pp37-50. – R. Roiphe/D. Cooper: Batman and the Jewish question, *NYT*, 2.7.92, p19. – P.D. Ryersson: Fine feathered friend: Danny DeVito interviewed, *Scarlet Street*, Winter 1993, p13. – P.D. Ryersson/M.O. Yaccarino: Bat beat, *Scarlet Street*, Winter 1993, p12. – M. Salberg etc: Anti-Semitism in BATMAN RETURNS? Be serious, *NYT*, 20.7.92, p14. – J. Schwager: Burton returns, *Boxoffice*, 6/1992, pp14-15. – B. Sharkey: Batman's city gets a new dose of urban blight, *NYT*, 14.6.92, pp13-14. – Mark Cotta Vaz: A knight at the zoo, *Cinefex*, 8/1992, pp22-69 [about the sepcial effects and computer animation]. – P.L. Walton: A slippage of masks: disguising Cat-Woman in BATMAN RETURNS, *Canadian Journal of Film Studies*, 1/1997, pp91-110. – Dominic Wells: Claws and effect, *Time Out*, 17.6.92, pp20-22. – T. White: Creating Catwoman, *Cf*, 2-3/1992, p10. **(fr:)** M. Ciment/L. Vachaud: La chauve-souris. Le chat et le pingouin, *Positif*, 9/1992, pp40-44. – B. Prayez: BATMAN – le défi, *Grand Angle*, 7/1992, pp17-18. – Yves Rousseau: Le carnaval des animaux, *24 Images*,

9-10/1992, pp87-89. **(ger:)** Franz Everschor: Ist Batmans Rückkehr antisemitisch?, *fd*, 18.8.92, p39. – Ingrid Kölle: Vor Batman gibt es nirgends ein Entkommen, *StZ*, 26.6.92. – Nicola Kuhn: Ein Fetisch für die kleinen Jungs – Mae West, Michelle Pfeiffer und der männliche Blick, *TSP*, 16.8.92. – Matthias Mattusek: Aufstand im Kinderzimmer, *Der Spiegel*, 27/1992, pp193-198. – Thomas Sieck: BATMAN RETURNS, *Enzyklopädie des phantastischen Films* (*Loseblattwerk*, 31. Erg. Lief., Sept. 1993).

THE NIGHTMARE BEFORE CHRISTMAS (1993)

Tie-in book: Frank Thompson: *Tim Burton's THE NIGHTMARE BEFORE CHRISTMAS — The Film, the Art, the Vision*, New York, 1993.

Reviews: **(eng:)** anon, *SI*, 16.7.93, p23. – D. Ansen, *Newsweek*, 1.11.93, p72. – T. Brownlie, *Film*, 1/1995, p23. – D. Denby, *New York Magazine*, 1.11.93, p74. – R. Ebert, *Chicago Sun-Times*, 22.10.93. – O. Gleiberman, *EW*, 22.10.93, p83. – E. Grant, *Films in Review*, 5-6/1994, p57. – R. Greene, *Boxoffice*, 12/1993. – J. Hoberman, *VV*, 19.10.93, p51. – K. Lally, *Film Journal*, 10-11/1993, p62. – J. Maslin, *NYT*, 9.10.93. – T. McCarthy, *Variety*, 18.10.93, p49. – K. Newman, *S&S*, 12/1993, pp53-54. – J. Painter, *Film Threat*, 6/1994, p58 [book review]. – G.J. Svehla, *Midnight Marquee*, Winter 1994, p87. – P. Travers, *Rolling Stone*, 11.11.93, pp79-80. – P. Warrick, *Modern Review*, 12-1/1994-1995, p18. **(fr:)** anon, *Mensuel du Cinéma*, 2/1994, p4. – M. de Blois, *24 Images*, 2-3/1994, pp78-79. – A. Caron, *Séquences*, 1/1994, pp43-44. – A. Caron, *Séquences*, 1-2/1995, pp49-50. – B. Génin, *Télérama*, 7.12.94, pp32-37. – T. Sotinel, *Le Monde*, 8.12.94. – Y. Tobin, *Positif*, 11/1994, p70. – L. Vachaud, *Positif*, 12/1994, pp6-7. **(ger:)** anon: *Der Spiegel*, 50/1994, p192. – Carl Andersen, *Neues Deutschland*, 8.12.94. – Bert Büllmann, *Cinema*, 12/1994, pp100-102. – Harald Fricke, *taz*, 15.12.94. – Bodo Fründt, *SZ*, 8.12.94. – Daniel Kothenschulte, *BerlZ*, 8.12.94. – Daniel Kothenschulte, *fd*, 6.12.94, pp24-25. – Detlev Kühn, *epd Film*, 1/1995, pp42-43. – Thomas Klingenmair, *StZ*, 8.12.94 – Sven Krügel, *BM*, 8.12.94. – Milan Pavlovic, *Steadycam*, Nr. 26 (1994), pp93-97. – Carla Rhode, *TSP*, 8.12.94.

Other sources: **(eng:)** Mimi Avins: Ghoul world, *Premiere* (USA), 11/1993, pp102-108. – P.E. Cole/R. Zoglin: Music from the dark side, *Time*, 11.10.93, pp80-81. – Richard Corliss etc: A sweet and scary treat, *Time*, 11.10.93, pp79-81. – Steve Dayle: Ghost in the machine: Tim Burton's animated NIGHTMARE haunts Disney with the question: 'Can naughty be nice?', *EW*, 29.10.93. – Joel Engel: *Screenwriters on Screenwriting*, New York, 1995 [interview with writer Caroline Thompson]. – Anna Everett: The other pleasures: The function of race in the cinema, *Film Criticism*, Autumn-Winter 1995/1996, pp26-38. – Leslie Felperin/Kim Newman: Animated dreams, *S&S*, 12/1994, pp26-29, 53-54 [including an interview with Henry Selick]. – Lawrence French: Animation Art Direction, *Cf*, 5/1993, p47. – L. French: Henry Selick, puppet director, *Cf*, 5/1993, p39. – L. French: Puppet Camerawork, *Cf*, 5/1993, pp40-41. – L. French:

Puppeteers as actors, *Cf*, 5/1993, pp32-33. – L. French: Puppetmaster Tim Burton, *Cf*, 5/1993, p34. – L. Kendall etc: The next great non-controversity: NIGHTMARE, *Film Score Monthly*, 11/1993, p14. – Nancy Griffin/Kim Masters: *Hit & Run. How Jon Peters and Peter Guber took Sony for a ride in Hollywood*, New York, 1996. – Pete Kozachik: Stop motion without compromise: NIGHTMARE, *AC*, 12/1993, pp37-43 [production diary]. – Roberta E. Pearson/William Uricchio (Ed): *The Many Lives of the Batman*, New York, 1991. – Stephen Rebello: Danny Elfman's NIGHTMARE, *Movieline*, 11/1993, pp55-58. – B. Sharkey: Tim Burton's NIGHTMARE comes true, *NYT*, 10.10.93. – Starburst, 2/1995, p24 [about the soundtrack]. – Mark Cotta Vaz: Animation in the third dimension, *Cinefex*, 11/1993, pp30-53. **(fr:)** Gilles Ciment: L'auteur, l'auteur! Henry Selick, Tim Burton et L'ÉTRANGE NOËL DE MONSIEUR JACK, *Positif*, 6/1995, pp86-90. – Thierry Jousse etc: L'ÉTRANGE NOËL de Tim Burton, *Cahiers*, 12/1994, pp22-32, 34-37. – Luc Moullet: La métamorphose, *Cahiers*, 7-8/1995, pp46-47. – N. Saada: Herrmann et son fils spirituel, *Cahiers*, 4/1995, p22 [about Bernard Herrmann and Elfman]. – J.-B. Thoret/A. Schlockoff: L'ÉTRANGE NOËL DE MONSIEUR JACK, *Écran Fantastique*, 12/1994-1/1995, pp7, 38-54.

ED WOOD (1994)

Biography: Rudolph Grey: *Nightmare of Ecstasy — The Life and Art of Edward D. Wood, Jr*, Portland, 1992.

Reviews: **(eng:)** R. Alleva, *Commonweal*, 2.12.94, pp13-14. – D. Ansen, *Newsweek*, 10.10.94, pp71-72. – J. Beebe, *San Francisco Young Institute Library Journal*, 1/1995, pp73-74. – J. Brennan, *LA Times*, 2.10.94. – M. Carducci, *Cf*, 2/1994, pp4-5. – P. N. Chuma, *Films in Review*, 9-10/1995, pp55-56. – R. Corliss, *Time*, 10.10.94, p82. – D. Denby, *New York Magazine*, 17.10.94, pp70-71. – R. Ebert, *Chicago Sun-Times*, 7.10.94. – P. Farrell, *Scarlet Street*, Autumn 1995, p41. – C. Gagne, *Film Journal*, 10-11/1994, pp73-74. – O. Gleiberman, *EW*, 14.10.94, p40. – T. Gliatto/L. Armstrong, *People*, 10.10.94. – R. Greene, *Boxoffice*, 11/1994. – J. Hoberman, *VV*, 4.10.94, p51. – A. Hultkrans, *Artforum*, 12/1994, pp11-12. – P. Klawans, *Nation*, 17.10.94, pp433-434. – K. Lewis, *Films in Review*, 1-2/1995, pp60-61. – T. Lucas, *Video Watchdog*, 1995, pp10-11. – T. McCarthy, *Variety*, 12.9.94, p39. – J. Matthews, *Newsday*, 28.9.94. – K. Newman, *S&S*, 5/1995, pp44-45 – D. Persons, *Cf*, 3/1995, p59. – T. Rafferty, *New Yorker*, 3.10.94, pp109-111. – F. Scheck, *Hollywood Reporter*, 23.9.94, pp10, 20. – M. Stimpson, *Film*, 3/1995, p20. – G.D. Sumner, *American History*, 5/1995, pp1206-1207. – P. Travers, *Rolling Stone*, 20.10.94, pp153, 155. – M. Wilmington, *LA Times*, 7.12.90. **(fr:)** J.P. Coursodon, *Positif*, 12/1994, pp8-11. – A. Dubeau, *Séquences*, 11-12/1994, pp24-25 and 1-2/1995, p45. – D. Dumas, *Avant Scène Cinéma*, 7/1995, p82. – I. Danel, *Télérama*, 21.6.95, pp34-37. - *Écran Fantastique*, 3/1996, p52. – M. Jean, *24 Images*, 12-1/1994-1995, pp60-61. – O. Kohn, *Positif*, 6/1995, pp15-17. – P. Mérigeau, *Le Monde*, 22.6.95. **(ger:)** Michael Althen, *Die Zeit*, 14.7.95. – Carl Andersen, *Neues Deutschland*, 20.7.95. – Frank Arnold, *BerlZ*, 13.7.95. – Bert Büllmann, *Cinema*, 7/1995, pp54-61. – Brigitte Desalm, *KStA*, 15.7.95. – Eberhard von Elterlein, *BM*, 13.7.95. – Eberhard von Elterlein, *Die Welt*, 13.7.95. – Ralph Eue, *tip*, 15/1995. – Fritz Göttler, *SZ*, 13.7.95. – Sabine Horst, *epd Film*, 7/1995, p34. – Sabine Horst, *FR*, 14.7.95. – Peter W. Jansen, *TSP*, 13.7.95. – Thomas Klingenmair, *StZ*, 13.7.95. – Heike Kühn, *Die Woche*,14.7.95. – Verena Lueken, *FAZ*, 15.7.95. – Hans Jörg Marsilius, *fd* 13/1995, pp24-25. – Helmut Merschmann, *Das Sonntagsblatt*, 14.7.95. – Hans-Joachim Neumann, *Zitty*, 14/1995. – Mariam Niroumand, *taz*, 13.7.95. – Georg Seeßlen, *epd Film*, 9/1995, pp4-7. – Martin Schlappner, *NZZ*, 30.6.95. – Volker Gunske, *tip*, 15/1995. – Angie Dullinger, *AZ*, 30.6.95.

Other sources: **(eng:)** anon: Landau and Lugosi meet Shakespeare, *Newsweek*, 10.10.94, p72. – G. Andrew: Hopeless pocus – Junk male, *Time Out*, 24.5.95, p22, 71. – V. Barajas: Knock on wood: Tim Burton films ED WOOD, *Scarlet Street*, Autumn 1994, pp50-54. – M. Carducci: Deadringer for Tor, *Cf*, 5/1994, pp26-27. – M. Carducci: Makeup, *Cf*, 5/1994, pp28-29. – M. Carducci: Flying Saucer Myths, *Cf*, 5/1994, p31. – J. Clark: The Wood, the Bad and the Ugly, *Premiere* (USA), 10/1994, pp90-94. – D. Edelstein: Tim Burton's Hollywood nightmare, *Vanity Fair*, 11/1994, p124. – L. French: Playing Bela Lugosi, *Cf*, 5/1994, pp24-25. – L. French: Tim Burton's ED WOOD, *Cf*, 5/1994, pp32-34. – D. Giammarco: Tim Burton's Plan 9 from Burbank, *Film Threat*, 4/1994, pp46-49. – O. Gleiberman: The awful truth in ED WOOD, *EW*, 30.9.94, p36. – Tom Gliatto: Master Ed, *People*, 31.10.94, pp87-88, 90. – C. Gore/J. Berg: Ed or Johnny?, *Film Threat*, 12/1994, pp36-39. – J. Hoberman/K. Newman: ED WOOD... not, *S&S*, 5/1995, pp10-12, 44-45. – David J. Hogan: ED WOOD: Original soundtrack recording, *Filmfax*, 5-6/1996, p26. – David Kipen: Bela of the ball, *Los Angeles Daily News*, 28.9.94. – Andy Klein: The famous Mr. Ed, *Los Angeles Reader*, 30.9.94, pp66, 68. – J. Lilley: Conrad Brooks on the set of ED WOOD, *Scarlet Street*, Winter 1994, pp21-22. – Bob Madison: Lugosi at the Academy Awards, *Scarlet Street*, Summer 1995, p19. – G. O'Brien: A kinder, gentler perversity, *New York Review of Books*, 17.11.94, pp19-20. – Steve Randisi: Inside the Wood Works. An interview with Conrad Brooks [actor in PLAN 9 FROM OUTER SPACE], *Filmfax*, 10-11/1994, pp62-67. – Steve Randisi: Bela's atomic bride, *Filmfax*, 5-6/1996, pp33-37. – Stephen Rebello: In Depp, *Movieline*, 10/1994, pp40-45, 81-82. – Paul M. Sammon: Wood works, *Cinefex*, 3/1995, pp107-110. – Don Shay: The return of the vampire, *Cinefex*, 12/1994, pp117-118. – Michail Stein: Landau's Lugosi, *Outré* (USA), 1994, pp28-34 [interview with Martin Landau]. – Kenneth Turan: ED WOOD: '50s blithe spirit, *LA Times*, 28.9.94. – Kenneth Turan: Up from Transylvania: Interview with Martin Landau, *The Valley Vantage*, 13.10.94. **(fr:)** C. Arnaud: ED WOOD ou l'avenir de l'homme, *Vertigo*, 14/1996, pp55-57. – Antoine Baecque: Changer de peau, *Vertigo*, 14/1996, p58. – Antoine Baecque/Bill Krohn: Wonder Wood – Le cas Wood, *Cahiers*, 6/1995, pp18-29 [including an interview with Landau]. – Sylvie Gendron/Alain Dubeau: ED WOOD: Appelez-le Ann

Gora, *Séquences*, 11-12/1994, pp21-25. – Cathy Karani: Le festival du vague à l'âme, *Écran Fantastique*, 7-8/1995, pp48-49. – Cathy Karani/Alain Schlockoff, Jean-Baptiste Thoret: ED WOOD [special section], *Écran Fantastique*, 5-6/1995, pp12-25. – B. Krohn: Entretien avec Martin Landau, *Cahiers*, 6/1995, pp24-29. **(ger:)** Frank Arnold: 'Einfach unterirdisch', *KStA*, 12.8.95 [interview with Ed Woods partner Dolores Fuller]. – Gunter Göckenjan: Dreck de luxe, *Die Woche*, 14.7.95 [on the comeback of trashy films]. – Roland Haschke: 'Tim Burton hat mich erpresst', *Cinema*, 7/1995, p61 [interview with Martin Landau]. – Hellmuth Karasek: Schlecht, schlechter, am schlechtesten, *Der Spiegel*, 20/1995, p230. – Thomas Klingenmair: Sternstunden der Unfähigkeit, *StZ*, 9.7.95. – Hans-Jörg Marsilius: Ed Wood. Ein skurriles Idol, *fd*, 14/1995, pp9-11. – Hans-Joachim Neumann: Naturtalent für schlechte Filme, *Zitty*, 14/1995.

MARS ATTACKS! (1996)

Tie-in books: Jonathan Gems: Mars Attacks! Der Roman zum Film, München, 1997 – Karen R. Jones: MARS ATTACKS! The Art of the Movie. London, Titan Books, 1996.

Reviews: **(eng:)** A. Bernstein, *Drama-Lounge*, 19.12.96. – P. Biodrowski, *Cf*, 10/1997, pp56-57. – M. Clark, *USA Today*, 29.10.96. – G. M. Dobbs, *Animato!*, Spring 1997, p4. – R. Ebert, *Chicago Sun-Times*, 13.12.96. – M. Ehrman, *LA Times*, 16.12.96. – A. C. Ferrante, *Fangoria*, 1/1997. – J. Garner, *Gannett News Service*, 10.12.96. – R. Granger, *Film Journal*, 1-2/1997, p83. – A. Hofman, *Jerusalem Post*, March 1997. – C. James, *Boxoffice*, 2/1997, p68. – T. McCarthy, *Variety*, 2.12.96, pp66-67. – K. Newman, *S&S*, 3/1997, pp53-54. – R. Novak, *People*, 23.12.96, pp17-18. – T. Rafferty, *New Yorker*, 16.12.96, pp116-118. – R. Schickel, *Time*, 23.12.96. – K. Turan, *LA Times*, 13.12.96. – B. Warren, *Starlog*, 1/1997. **(fr:)** M. de Blois, *24 Images*, Spring 1997, pp46-48. – O. Clinckart, *Grand Angle*, 3/1997, pp29-30. – H. Gervin, *Séquences*, 1-2/1997, pp49-51. – R. Lamy, *Jeune Cinéma*, 3-4/1997, pp38-39. – N. Saada, *Cahiers*, 3/1997, pp72-73. – C. Viviani, *Positif*, 3/1997, pp6-8. **(ger:)** Frank Arnold, *epd Film*, 3/1997, pp32-33. – Lars-Olav Beier, *FAZ*, 22.2.97. – Eberhard von Elterlein, *Die Welt*, 27.2.97. – Franz Everschor, *fd*, 4/1997, p20. – Gunter Göckenjan, *BerlZ*, 22.2.97. – Urs Jenny, *Der Spiegel*, 10/1997, pp196. – Rupert Koppold, *StZ*, 27.2.97. – Martina Lange, *Die Woche*, 28.2.97. – Angelika Mihan, *Märkische Allgemeine*, 27.2.97. – Milan Pavlovic, *Steadycam*, Nr. 33 (1997), p87. – Heiko Rosner, *Cinema*, 3/1997, pp34-49. – Claudius Seidl, *SZ*, 27.2.97. – Dominik Slappnig, *Zoom*, 3/1997, p43. – Dieter Strunz, *BM*, 23.2.97. – Christoph Terhechte, *tip*, 4/1997.

Other sources: **(eng:)** anon: MARS ATTACKS!, *S&S*, 2/1997, pp6-9 [comparison with INDEPENDENCE DAY]. – Jeff Bond: Still more Jeff Bond..., *Film Score Monthly*, 3/1997, pp34-38 [about the soundtrack]. – Karl Cohen: How to animate an alien, *Animato!*, Spring 1997, pp16-17, 56. – Denis Ferrara/St. Clair Pugh: Sidney: To Mars and back, *LA Times*, 24.6.96. – Marshall

Fine: MARS ATTACKS! trades too much for too little, *Gannett News Service*, 13.12.96. – Don Groves: MARS out of the world: Burton's pic hits stride at o'seas B.O, *Daily Variety*, 10.3.97, pp12, 14. – L. Kendall: Lukas attacks! In: *Film Score Monthly*, 12/1996, pp21-23 [about the soundtrack]. – R.D. Larson: MARS ATTACKS!, *Soundtrack!*, 6/1997, p57 [about the soundtrack]. – Ron Magid: Strange invaders. Effects enhance lunacy of MARS ATTACKS! Scenario, *AC*, 12/1996, pp50-57. – Robert Marich: MARS ATTACKS! – More weird from Tim Burton, *Gannett News Service*, 13.12.96. – Peter Rainer: It's topps!, *Los Angeles New Times*, 12.12.96, pp26, 30. – David T. Rice: MARS ATTACKS! – Every picture tells a story, *Outré* (USA), I/7, 1997, pp44-52. – Andrew Roberts: Gems Attacks, *Fade In*, II/3, 1996, pp48-49. – Frederick C. Szebin/Steve Biodrowski: Interview with Danny Elfman, *Soundtrack!*, 3/1997, pp4-7. – Frederick C. Szebin/P. Biodrowski: MARS ATTACKS!, *Cf*, 10/1997, pp18-30. – M.C. Vaz: Martial art, *Cinefex*, 12/1996, pp70-93. – C. Wagner: Martian Inspiration, *Cf*, 7/1997, pp19-21. – D. E. Williams: Galactic antics. MARS ATTACKS! adds camp spin to alien invasion, *AC*, 12/1996, pp40-49. – William Woof: In praise of Tim Burton: Finding the masterpiece in MARS ATTACKS!, *Kinema*, Spring 1998. **(fr:)** Samuel Blumenfeld: A bien des égards. MARS ATTACKS! est une métaphore de la guerre de Golfe, *Le Monde*, 27.2.97. – Caroline Thompson: Le travail avec Tim Burton, *Positif*, 3/1997, pp12-13. – M. Jean: Carnet de notes sur le corps martien, *24 Images*, Spring 1997, pp10-11. – R. Simons: The Sound of Music, *Grand Angle*, April 1997, pp61-62 [about theoundtrack]. **(ger:)** Markus Tschiedert: 'Mein Kopf fühlte sich an, als ob er gleich explodieren würde', *Moviestar*, 4/1997, p37 [interview with Lisa Marie]. – Bill Warren: Unsere liebsten Marsmännchen greifen an!, *Starlog*, 8/1996, pp24-29.

SLEEPY HOLLOW (1999)

Reviews/Other sources: **(eng:)** Tim Burton's Sleepy Hollow: Director Burton on his poetic ode to Hammer horror, with Johnny Depp as Ichabod Crane, in their third collaboration, *Cf*, Dec. 1999. – Roger Ebert, *Chicago Sun-Times*, 19.11.99. – Richard Corliss: Tim Burton's Tricky Treat, *Time*, 22.11.99. – Jeff Giles: The Headless Horseman rides again, *Newsweek*, 22.11.99. – Vanessa Grigoriadis: Hollow man, *New York Magazine*, 22.11.99. – Chris Grunden, *Film Journal*, Dec. 1999. – J. Hoberman: Heads or tails, *VV*, 24.11.99. – Mick LaSalle: SLEEPY HOLLOW a Yawner. Burton's direction is a true horror, *San Francisco Chronicle*, 19.11.99. – Todd McCarthy: SLEEPY HOLLOW, *Variety*, 15.11.99. – Wesley Morris: Hats off to 'Sleepy Hollow', *San Francisco Examiner*, 19.11.99. – Lorenza Munoz: Awakening Burton's 'Sleepy' vision, *LA Times*, 22.11.99. – Stephen Pizzelo: Galloping ghost, *AC*, Dec. 1999. – Jonathan Rosenbaum: Hollow rendition, *Chicago Reader*, 19.11.99. – Kenneth Turan: Heads roll in 'Hollow' that's darker than ever, *LA Times*, 19.11.99.

Bibliography: Maurice Lahde

Index

Also available from Titan Books:

Joel & Ethan Coen

by Peter Körte and Georg Seesslen

Joel & Ethan Coen is the first in-depth analysis of the critically acclaimed Coen brothers' work, providing detailed coverage of all their movies, from Sam Raimi's *Crimewave* to the award-winning *The Big Lebowski*. The brothers' many success- es also include their breathtaking directorial début *Blood Simple*, cult favourite *Raising Arizona*, Cannes winner *Barton Fink* and box office hit *Fargo*. For the first time, each of the Coens' films is painstakingly examined, focusing on their unique visual imagination, razor-sharp dialogue and quirky plots, and including:

● over five hundred photographs
● an exclusive interview with both Joel and Ethan Coen
● a complete credits listing for every Coen brothers film

The Coen brothers' movies continue to intrigue audiences and critics alike, and *Joel & Ethan Coen* is the definitive look at one of the most inventive film-making teams of the last twenty years.